MISSION-BASED MARKETING

SECOND EDITION

AN ORGANIZATIONAL DEVELOPMENT WORKBOOK

PETER C. BRINCKERHOFF

A companion to *Mission-Based Marketing,*
Second Edition

WILEY

Contents

Preface

After the first edition of *Mission-Based Marketing* was published in 1997, I received many comments from readers about how they liked the practical nature of the book—particularly, the hands-on nature of the suggestions. In 2000, I published a second edition of my first book, *Mission-Based Management,* as well as a companion workbook. The response to the paired book update and hands-on workbook was overwhelmingly positive.

As the second edition of *Mission-Based Marketing* was being contemplated, it became obvious that a companion volume was also needed to help mission-based managers like you fully implement the suggestions, ideas, and concepts in the book. Thus came this *Mission-Based Marketing Workbook,* which I sincerely hope will help you in your efforts to get your organization on the road to becoming and remaining a market-driven, mission-based not-for-profit.

I wish you the best in your reading and in your application of the ideas in *Mission-Based Marketing*. I know, from both my own experience and from the feedback of thousands of not-for-profit managers, that the ideas work and that they result in better organizations doing more missions. Of course, not every idea works for every organization in every circumstance—nor will any of the ideas serve as a panacea for a dysfunctional organization. But for most organizations in most situations, the vast majority of the concepts and ideas can help you tremendously.

About the Author

Peter Brinckerhoff is an internationally acclaimed consultant, lecturer, and award-winning author. He is president of Corporate Alternatives, Inc., the consulting firm that he founded in 1982. He is a former staff member, executive director, board member, and volunteer for local, state, and national not-for-profit organizations.

Peter is the author of nine books on not-for-profit management issues, all part of the *Mission-Based Management Series* published by John Wiley & Sons.

Peter lives in Springfield, Illinois with his wife and three children.

1

Introduction:
How to Get the Most Out of
This Workbook

Welcome. This workbook is intended for the staff and board members of not-for-profit organizations as a hands-on tool to get more missions out the door by identifying your markets, picking which markets are your most important, asking your markets what they want, matching those wants with your core competencies to focus on what you do best, and in general to improve your overall mission capability. This workbook is really a tool to help you implement the ideas in *Mission-Based Marketing* in the easiest, quickest, and most efficient manner.

In this first chapter, I want to make sure that you understand how to get the most out of your investment in this workbook. I begin by making the assumption that you and your marketing team have read *Mission-Based Marketing*, preferably its second edition. While a first edition reader will find excellent value in this workbook, he or she might be a bit confused by the chapter sequencing of the workbook, which is designed to coordinate with the second edition's updated list of key criteria of success for a mission-based, market-driven organization.

Having said that, I assume that you want to get more out of *Mission-Based Marketing* and that you want the tools to implement ideas from the book quickly and efficiently. If so, you've come to the right place. This workbook is filled with hands-on tools, checklists, forms, and displays to bring the concepts home and to help you implement them in your organization smoothly and as soon as possible.

To that end, let's start by going through the organization of the workbook and its chapters. Then, I'll give you a few suggestions for using the tools included to the best effect.

A. ORGANIZATION

Immediately following this chapter is a chapter about leading group discussions. I include this information because the absolute best way to implement ideas like the ones in *Mission-Based Marketing* is in teams. Thus, you or one of your marketing team members will perform a lot of group facilitation. Chapter 2, "Getting Your Team Started," will help you get started if you have never done this activity, and will help you hone your skills if you have.

Chapter 3, "Benchmarking Your Organization: A Baseline Assessment Tool," takes you through the next step: benchmarking. I include a self-assessment form that enables you to review your organization against my criteria for marketing success and even give yourself a preliminary grade in each area. Before you spend a lot of time and money implementing my ideas, make sure to take the time to benchmark. It will focus you on where your needs are the greatest and motivate any members of your organization who do not think that there are ways to improve the organization.

Starting with Chapter 4, "Organizational Flexibility," each chapter covers one main topic, and they coordinate with the chapter of the same number in *Mission-Based Marketing*. The major components of each chapter are:

1. Straight from *Mission-Based Marketing*

First, we briefly review the key concepts included in *Mission-Based Marketing*. This review will not only refresh your memory but also underscore which things are the most important to consider in the topic under discussion. It will also help bring all the members of your marketing team to the same level if some of those team members have not read the book.

2. Baseline Self-Assessment

Although you should have already completed a full organizational self-assessment, I include an expanded, topic-specific assessment tool here for two reasons. First, the self-assessments in the chapters are significantly more detailed than those in Chapter 3, and they offer you more potential avenues for improvement. Second, some readers will eschew the organization-wide self-assessment included in Chapter 3 and will only read the chapters that cover the topics of their most intense interests. The self-assessment tools in the chapters will also enable you to grade your organization on a scale to give you an overall sense of where your organization stands.

☞ **HANDS-ON:** In all of my books, I include numerous practical suggestions highlighted by the ☞ **HANDS-ON:** icon that is so familiar to my readers. I have reiterated all the hands-on suggestions from each chapter in *Mission-Based Marketing* to give you some additional food for thought as you consider the best actions to take for your organization. These are nearly all immediately implementable ideas and will help you take some immediate action.

3. Worksheets and Checklists

The meat of the chapters is always here. I provide a series of worksheets and checklists to walk you through the steps of organizational improvement for each topic. Many of the worksheets are self-explanatory. When they are not, I will include instructions. Some of the worksheets stand alone, but many are provided in an intentional sequence and build on one another. This situation is particularly true in the areas of market identification and marketing planning.

At the end of each chapter's group of forms and checklists is a blank implementation checklist to help you set deadlines for getting things done and for assigning people the responsibilities of implementation.

4. Forms on the Companion CD-ROM

Most of the forms are also provided to you on the companion CD-ROM. This chart lists the form by exhibit number, name, page, and filename on the CD-ROM. I urge you to print out copies of the forms in the book or make duplicates from the book itself. You will hopefully be working with a team, and you will want to have multiple copies. I give you express permission to copy these forms for work by your organizational marketing team.

5. Resources for Further Study

In my books, I put the resources in the back, after the text. Here, I include them right in the chapters to make it easier for you to focus on the topic at hand and to find more help if necessary.

B. HOW TO USE THE WORKBOOK

I have four suggestions on how to work your way through the workbook to the best effect. If efficient, effective outcomes are what you are looking for, consider these four as rules, not just suggestions.

1. Read *Mission-Based Marketing* First

I know, I know, you want to get started. You don't have the time to read. But you need to understand that this workbook is designed as an implementation tool, not as a complete reiteration of all the background, examples, ideas, rationalizations, and encouragement in *Mission-Based Marketing*. If you want to "get it," read the book first.

2. Work as a Team

After 20 years of consulting and training, my favorite quote regarding the value of teamwork—and on the importance of sharing information widely—still is from John Chambers, the CEO of Cisco Systems. Chambers says, "No one of us is as smart as all of us." You are going to suggest change, sometimes very dramatic change, in your organization as a result of the ideas in this workbook. You need a team to realize that change. Using such a team to decide which ideas are for your organization, and enlisting the team's help in getting over the many barriers to implementation, is the best way to proceed. The team should include your key management staff but also representatives from your board of directors and your mid-management and line staff. Nine to 12 people are about right for this group, with others being brought in for ad-hoc input on areas of specific expertise. Make the team as broadly representative as you can.

3. Perform the Self-Assessment as a Group

For the workbook as a whole, and for each chapter in particular, start with the self-assessment. Make multiple copies and have the group fill them in independently which assures more objectivity and reduces the likelihood of one strong member of the group skewing the assessments. Then, get back together and compile the assessments noting the range (the high and low) for each item and the average.

Performing the self-assessment as a group will also give you a great opportunity for initial (and sometimes extended) discussion about the topic at hand. You will find out quickly about the perspectives of the group and where more education or information dissemination on the topic is needed.

4. Set a Measurable Outcome and a Deadline for Implementation, and Assign Responsibility

The last form in each chapter's section on forms and checklists is designed to help you here. As with any activity, if you don't set a measurable outcome, how can you tell whether you succeeded? If you don't set a deadline, because work expands to fill the time allotted, you will never get done. And unless you tell someone or some group that an activity is their job, it will always be someone else's. Fill in the implementation form, and enforce your expectations of outcome.

Here's another hint. If you move through the entire workbook, filling out all the implementation forms in each chapter, you will have a *Mission-Based Marketing* action plan ready just by collating the forms and passing them out to your key staff and board. Then, you can see how the organization can move ahead to be the market-driven, mission-based business that you need it to be.

As you move toward that goal, I wish you nothing but good times and excellent meetings, in comfortable surroundings with a good cappuccino for everyone. But I know that is not reality. Most readers are faced with many demands on their time and many more mission demands on their resources. You might well be highly stressed, distracted, and under a lot of pressure to make significant improvements in a short time. The workbook is designed to help just that kind of manager in just that kind of situation. By starting with the self-assessments, you can get a good idea of where you are. By using the forms and worksheets, you can detail specific outcomes and show progress in improving your organization. On crazy days, when you have to check your ID to merely remember your name (much less have a creative idea) the checklists can focus your thoughts and get you back on track.

Also, you need to be on the track toward becoming that market-driven, mission-based organization that you, your staff and board and—most importantly—the people who you serve need you to be. As always, the mission is the bottom line. But by using the marketing tools that I show you here, you can focus your resources to get more and better missions out the door. Good luck.

2

Getting Your Team Started

The core concept of this workbook is that you should use its forms, checklists, and decision trees to make progress in implementing ideas and suggestions from *Mission-Based Marketing* ideas *as a group*. While any manager needs to have the capacity to make decisions on his or her own, most of the concepts in *Mission-Based Marketing* require organizational change—often of such a large proportion that the best way to implement them is with a group.

In their good form, groups usually come up with consensus ideas. Groups can ameliorate ideas that are so radical that they are unworkable for an organization given its culture or its financial condition. Groups can share the workload. Groups can solve problems well. Remember my quote from John Chambers of Cisco Systems in the first chapter? "None of us is as smart as all of us."

Groups in their bad form can delay action, tear down new ideas, or force a continuation of the "same old same old." They can protect turf and turn really good, but a bit radical, ideas that will enhance the mission into boring, vanilla initiatives that will never motivate anyone.

Thus, as a leader of a mission-based organization, you need to work with groups and get the good things out of them quickly, efficiently, and with at least a bit of consensus. This chapter helps you along that path.

A. STRAIGHT FROM *MISSION-BASED MANAGEMENT*

No, this head is *not* a typo. I really want you to consider these ideas from *Mission-Based Management,* because they are so important to why and how you need to proceed with your marketing.

1. The More Information that People Have about the Organization, the Better

More than any other idea in the book, this topic pertains to the concept of including people in the decision-making process and informing them of the outcomes of different committee deliberations. Don't try to do all the heavy lifting yourself. Include people from throughout all levels of the organization in your *Mission-Based Marketing* team, and inform everyone of the group's progress and deliberations. A number of my clients put the minutes of all their various staff and board committees on part of their web site that can only be accessed by board and staff members. This feature enables the staff to keep up to speed on what is going on throughout the organization.

2. The Line Staff Are the Most Important Employees; Management Is a Support Function

You need to use an inverted pyramid management style, where the most important people are the line staff. As part of that philosophy, as you implement these ideas put people from your line staff, and representatives of your mid management levels, on your *Mission-Based Marketing* team. Also, of course, do the same for your other committees. If line staff are important, get their input. If you want to grow your own stars internally, start now. Let them gain a bigger picture of the organization by participating in bigger issues (learning how to be part of organizational leadership).

3. Mission-Based Managers Lead from the Front

Yes, you need input. Yes, you need a group to give you a variety of perspectives. But, on some issues, after getting the input you just have to make the decision and move ahead. In other words, lead. Examples of decisions that you might have to make are: We *are* going to be market-driven and mission-based. We *are* going to ask all of our customers what they think of us. We *are* going to have everyone on the marketing team. We *are* going to think of all of our markets as valued customers. Once such decisions have been made, you can move the organization ahead. Max DuPree, in his excellent book *Leading Without Power*, notes that most not-for-profits "spend far too much time going for consensus rather than going for agreement." I concur completely. After you have your ideas, input, suggestions, and discussion, make the decision and then ask: "We're going such and such a direction. Are you coming with us?"

B. ASSEMBLING AND USING YOUR *MISSION-BASED MARKETING* TEAM

1. A Mission-Based Marketing Implementation Process

When you use this workbook, I would suggest that you use the following sequence of activity:

a. Assemble your Mission-Based Marketing Team

I strongly recommend that you do two things with potential team members before you recruit them. First, talk to them privately to see whether they are interested and enthusiastic about helping. Then, find out whether they have major work conflicts that will keep them from attending meetings or getting their reading done on time. Make sure that they will be good team members. Second, don't select people just by title. Get the best people in your organization to work through these issues but not necessarily only those who have lots of experience in marketing or sales. Make sure that you find people who are close to your customers, people who understand your organizational strengths and weaknesses, and people who deal with both happy and unhappy customers.

b. Read the appropriate chapter in **Mission-Based Marketing**

You might want to perform this activity chapter by chapter or go through the entire workbook in a marathon session and coordinate the activities intended to implement priority ideas from each chapter. I suspect that you will get more out of your group if you go through a chapter at a time.

c. Meet and discuss the discussion questions at the end of each chapter

Weekly meetings help keep up the momentum. Certainly, you will lose your "mo" if you meet less than twice a month. Try to set all of the meeting dates at the first session, and try for a consistent time and place (e.g., second and fourth Mondays at 10 A.M.). Then, the team can have all the meetings on its calendar far in advance and there will be less conflict. Use your internal e-mail to regularly remind people of upcoming meetings.

d. Go through the forms and checklists in the workbook

(Remember: you are specifically allowed to copy these forms, and you can make originals from the accompanying disk.) Make sure that you copy all the forms on the CD-ROM before the meeting so that you can distribute them. Think about customizing the forms at the meeting to make them fit your needs better. You can add your organization's name to the forms or include specific services or markets.

e. Fill out your implementation checklist (the final form in each chapter's section)

Some chapters have forms that are pretty all-inclusive. Others call for work that should go on your implementation checklist. In many cases, you will think of things to improve that will not be on any of the lists. Make sure that the task gets on this overall implementation checklist. You might want to ask some member of your marketing team to edit the forms as you meet and then print them out in the newer, more complete format for your team.

f. Monitor your progress toward completion

Process is important, but product is what you are shooting for. Set outcomes, set deadlines, assign responsibilities, and then enforce your expectations. Also, you might want to be publicly accountable during this process. Share what the team is doing by posting the minutes of your meetings on the staff-only section of your web site. Share potential changes in written materials, or ask for ideas with wider groups of board and staff in-between meetings to spread the network widely for good ideas. People in the organization will be interested in (and some will be worried about) what your team is doing so keep them informed.

2. Rules for Facilitators

Most meetings need a leader or a facilitator. The facilitator of your meetings might or might not be the person who convenes the team and the meetings. A good facilitator is essential to getting the most out of the time that the team will spend together. Let's first review some key rules for facilitators and then look at how they can be used in your meetings (these come from Ron Myers, a strategic planning consultant based in New York):

- Agree on the objectives of the meeting.
- Establish a time frame for the meeting.
- Stick to the subject. Don't let people wander off the subject at hand, or you will lose the objectives and time frame.
- Provide new input only; no repetition of old ideas or ones that have already been discussed in the meeting.
- Focus on the bottom line first. Focus on important matters and fill in details later.
- Have one conversation at a time. Squelch side conversations. Keep people focused on the speaker who has the floor.
- Prohibit snide remarks.
- Silence is consent. A person who does not speak up is assumed to consent to the group's decision.

Ron also has a great way to keep the group on track. Put a bowl in the middle of the table. Anyone who wanders off the subject, repeats something clearly said before, engages in a side conversation, or makes a snide remark puts money into the bowl (the amount can vary; a quarter or a dollar). The group as a whole is quick to call out when someone transgresses the rules. It serves to keep the group focused. The money buys refreshments for the next meeting.

Now, let's look at how these eight suggestions apply to your team.

1. Consider the choice of facilitator carefully. It might not be best to have the executive director or CEO be in charge of the meeting. You need someone who can move the discussion along but not dominate the group. If the executive director is not the facilitator, the person who does the facilitating must be strong enough to cut the executive off if he or she starts to control the agenda.
2. Prior to the meeting, the facilitator must have thoroughly read the assignment and should have reviewed the discussion questions suggested in *Mission-Based Marketing* and the worksheets and checklists included in this workbook, deciding which to use. Any additional questions that might be important for the organization should also be written down. Copies of the questions to be asked should be distributed to members of the team. Also, if there are any materials that are going to be reviewed at the meetings (policies, mission statement, and so on), these should be gathered prior to the meeting. Finally, the facilitator should assure that some means for writing down the work of the team is available. This task might mean a chalk or white board, a flip chart, or someone taking notes.
3. At the beginning of each meeting, the facilitator should review the time allotted for the meeting and what issues will be covered. The questions to be discussed can be distributed at this point, or the facilitator might want to simply ask the questions as the meeting progresses. This decision depends on the facilitator's style. In any case, everyone should agree on the objectives of the meeting and the subjects to be discussed. A time frame (deadline for adjournment) should also be reiterated. This topic should have been discussed in advance, but it never hurts to remind people.

4. The facilitator should start with the "key philosophy" and end with the "implementation checklist" for each chapter. This discussion will focus and then wrap up the discussion well.

5. The facilitator should work to encourage discussion on all sides of an issue and to assure that everyone present has a chance to voice their views. While the rules of facilitation note that "silence is consent," I have found that there is always someone who wants to bring up the opposite view, but often they are afraid. What I say is, "It seems we all agree that this is the way to go, but I am concerned that we haven't looked at the down side. What are the possible negative results of this action?" Then, I empower the person who would have been seen as a "nay-sayer." He or she has just been transformed from a whiner to a good manager. He or she gets the chance to contribute and thus to have ownership in the final decision. This person also often brings up important ideas that the group would not have heard. Ultimately, however, if people are unwilling to contribute, they have consented to the will of the group.

   Work to keep only new ideas on the table, and don't let people repeat the same ideas over and over or make snide remarks about "wild ideas" that "won't work here." Use the bowl.

6. The facilitator should write down decisions and ideas developed by the group. I like using an easel and newsprint pad so that everyone can see what is being written down. This feature documents ideas and enables people to further brainstorm. Some facilitators like to have someone else as their "scribe" so that they can concentrate on keeping the group moving. Either way is fine.

7. Try to get through as many questions on the list as possible in each meeting, but don't go over the time allotted without complete concurrence from everyone there. For each question, focus on what changes or actions need to be taken to improve the organization, who should make them, and what deadline is appropriate. Again, remember that there is an implementation checklist provided in each chapter.

8. Remember, your meeting should probably not last more than 90 minutes. At the end of each session, reserve 10 minutes to review the decisions made, their deadlines, and who is responsible to make them happen. Have this information written up and distributed in writing, by e-mail or on your web site, to the participants within 24 hours. Remind everyone of the next meeting date and assignment before adjourning.

C. RESOURCES FOR FURTHER STUDY

Topic: Meeting Facilitation and Leadership
Books
Working Together: 55 Team Games by Lorraine L. Ukens. Jossey-Bass, 1996. (ISBN 078790354X).   *The Skilled Facilitator: A Comprehensive Resource for Consultants, Facilitators, Managers, Trainers, and Coaches* by Roger Schwarz. Jossey-Bass, 1994. (ISBN 0787947237).   *A Practical Guide to Needs Assessment* by Kavita Gupta. Jossey-Bass, 1998. (ISBN 0787939889).
Software
Haven't seen any of this kind of software yet, but it won't be long (perhaps even by the time you read this book). Check out a site such as *www.cnet.com*.
Web Sites
boardsource.com   *www.missionbased.com*
Education
One of the sites with all the higher ed.   **Nonprofit Education:** This site is the most complete for nonprofit academic programs all over North America. Check out the institutions to find the most up-to-date online offerings, which are increasing every month: *http://pirate.shu.edu/~mirabero/Kellogg.html*

3

Benchmarking Your Organization: A Baseline Assessment Tool

So, let's get started. First things first, I provide you with a hands-on baseline assessment tool that will help you and your *Mission-Based Marketing* team take an initial look at the status of your organization in relation to my criteria for success and my suggestions in the book. Take the time to fill in this survey as a group. Then, you can focus your efforts on the parts of your organization that can most benefit from your time and efforts.

A. STRAIGHT FROM *MISSION-BASED MARKETING*

I just have to start with the big philosophies from *Mission-Based Marketing* as a starting point. You need to read these aloud as a group and talk them through. If your *Mission-Based Marketing* team agree on these, you are going to make excellent changes. If there is disagreement about the underlying concepts, you need to know it *before* you start, not after. *Mission-Based Marketing* hinges on these five ideas:

1. Everything that Everyone in Your Organization Does Every Day Is Marketing

There is nowhere to hide from this concept. Every staff member and volunteer contributes (or detracts) from your organization's image in the community. Marketing is a team sport, and everyone is always playing. Remind your staff that when they are happy (or unhappy) with a retail transaction, they are nearly always happy (or unhappy) with the actions of one of the lowest-paid workers, not with the CEO or director of marketing.

2. It's All About Wants, Not Needs

In the not-for-profit sector, we constantly pat ourselves on the back because we fill needs in the community. While this is fine, we must also remember that in order to get people what they *need*, we have to give it to them in a way that they *want* it. All of us have needs. All of us seek wants. Don't confuse the two.

3. Ask, Ask, and Ask and Then Listen

To find out what people want, you have to ask and ask regularly. The biggest mistake that people make in marketing (other than confusing needs and wants) is saying, "I've been in this field for 20 years, and I know what people want." Here is the truth: no one knows what anyone wants unless he or she has asked and asked recently. People are fickle, and their wants are constantly changing. Ask, and then make sure that you listen to what they want.

4. Customers Never Have Problems, Only Crises

We need to look at things through our customers' eyes and have a sense of compassionate urgency about what we do for them. Remember my friend the cardiologist's reminder to his staff: "What we do every day is a once in a lifetime experience for our patients. We need to never forget that." Good advice. Empower your staff to act, to act with compassion and expertise, and to act quickly. In our part of the world, nearly all the people who come through our doors have problems of one kind or another. Even if we see 10,000 similar people every year, each of them deserves to be treated as an individual with a sensitivity to their urgent needs and wants.

5. With Price, the Issue Is Never Cost: It Is Always about Value

If the issue was only price, we wouldn't have Rolls Royce automobiles, first-class airline seats, or Ritz Carleton hotels. No one would pay $50 for a regular season baseball game ticket or spend $5,000 at an auction for used (also known as antique) furniture. But they (and we) do. Why? We value the product or service enough. Put another way, we get what we want. What value does your organization provide to your clients, funders, staff, and volunteers? Is the value seen as that by your customers? Remember, value is always from the perspective of the customer.

B. BASELINE SELF-ASSESSMENT

To make plans for the future, you must know where you are in the present. These self-assessment pages are designed to help you, your staff, and your board diagnose the current situation of your organization in relation to my suggestions and ideas in *Mission-Based Marketing*. The sections follow the chapters in the book.

This self-assessment tool can be used in many ways. One of the best ways is to conduct a retreat or workshop involving key organization leaders. Or you can use it at the first meeting of your *Mission-Based Marketing* team. At the session, provide each participant with the self-assessment pages and with a copy of *Mission-Based Marketing*. Then, begin the session by going through the self-assessment (referring to the book as needed). Invite open discussion. Encourage an honest and fair assessment. Don't squelch the negative assessments. After all, no organization can be perfect. The self-assessment discussion will be helped by having a large pad of paper on an easel or a chalk board. The facilitator can write down comments that indicate areas needing attention. Also, you can score your organization and see where you need the most improvement. If you score on the low side in a certain section, don't panic. Set some goals for short-term improvement.

Remember to have each of the most critical items assigned to a person to follow through on. A timetable should be established for each item. This list of top-priority items, the person responsible for each, and the date or dates for taking the key steps to deal with the item should be recorded. This list will be a record of the outcomes of the session—outcomes that will lead to actions where the organization's leaders have diagnosed areas for improvement through this self-assessment.

Instructions: Go through each area of the self-evaluations (Forms 3-1 to 3-9). For each question, circle the box with the score next to the question. Then, total your scores in each column, add the "yes" and "no" columns together, and put the resulting total score in the appropriate box for each subject. A score can be positive, negative, or 0. For example, if you have a yes answer for the first question under Mission Statement, you get a **2.** A no answer gets a **–2**. A "perfect" mission score would generate a score of **13.** A **–5** would be generated if all the answers were no.

Form 3-1 **Flexibility (Chapter 4)**		
	Yes	**No**
Are we doing just the same services in the same way as three years ago?	2	–2
Is change considered an opportunity to improve, as opposed to a threat to the status quo?	3	–1
Did we make money in each of the past three years as an organization?	3	–1
Is at least 5 percent of our income unrestricted?	2	–1
Are we concerned about regular small improvements in services?	3	0
Total of Column Score (Add up each column and put the answer here.) ➜		
TOTAL SCORE—MISSION (Add total scores from Yes and No columns and put the answer here.) ➜		

● FORM0301.DOC

Form 3-2 The Marketing Cycle (Chapter 5)

	Yes	No
Do we identify our markets before we figure out what they want?	3	−3
Do we know our three key (target) payer markets?	3	0
Do we know our three key (target) service markets?	3	0
Do we consider how we provide services in light of what these markets want?	3	−1
Do we promote our services and products to meet wants as opposed to needs?	2	−1
Are we stuck in a *needs assessment* only mode, or do we really consider what our service recipients *want*?	3	−3
Do we review the prices we can control every six months?	2	0
Do we have an evaluation component to our marketing effort?	3	0
Total of Column Score (Add up each column and put the answer here.) ➜		
TOTAL SCORE—MARKETING CYCLE (Add total scores from Yes and No columns and put the answer here.) ➜		

● FORM0302.DOC

Form 3-3 Your Markets (Chapter 6)		
	Yes	No
Do we know who all of our funder markets are?	3	–1
Do we know who all of our referral markets are?	3	–1
Do we know who all of our service recipient markets are?	3	–1
Have we developed two to five target markets in each of the above three areas?	4	–2
Have we assigned a member of our marketing team to be the key liason/expert for each target market?	3	–1
Have we gathered baseline data on all of our internal and external markets?	2	–1
Do we regularly check to see how our target markets have changed?	3	–1
Total of Column Score (Add up each column and put the answer here.) →		
TOTAL SCORE (Add total scores from Yes and No columns and put the answer here.) →		

FORM0303.DOC

Form 3-4   Who Are Your Competitors? (Chapter 7)

	Yes	No
Have we identified our competitors for each of our target markets?	3	–1
Have we researched our competitors' strengths?	2	0
Have we identified our competitors' weaknesses?	2	0
Are we focusing on the same target markets as our competitors?	2	–1
Do we ask our network of board, staff, vendors, and funders about our competitors?	3	–1
Do we view competition as an inherently good thing?	4	–1
Total of Column Score (Add up each column and put the answer here.) ➜		
TOTAL SCORE (Add total scores from Yes and No columns and put the answer here.) ➜		

● FORM0304.DOC

Form 3-5 Asking Your Markets (Chapter 8)

	Yes	No
Do we ask our payers about their satisfaction with us at least annually?	3	0
Do we ask our service customers about their satisfaction with us at least annually?	3	0
Do we ask our staff about their job satisfaction at least every 18 months?	3	0
Do we ask our board about their satisfaction at least every 18 months?	3	0
Do we have a culture of asking?	2	–1
Do we train our staff in how to ask and how to listen?	2	0
Total of Column Score (Add up each column and put the answer here.) ➔		
TOTAL SCORE (Add total scores from Yes and No columns and put the answer here.) ➔		

● FORM0305.DOC

Form 3-6 **Better Marketing Materials (Chapter 9)**	Yes	No
Do we focus on one general purpose brochure?	–4	2
Do we have targeted materials for our three top payer markets?	3	–1
Do we have targeted materials for our three top service markets?	3	–2
Do we have printed materials that focus on our referral sources?	3	–3
Is all of our marketing material reviewed and updated at least anually?	3	–2
Does all of our marketing material include contact name, phone number, website, and e-mail information?	4	–3
Do we have a web site?	5	–5
Is our web site checked every 30 days for currency?	2	–2
Do we have special sections on our web site for board, staff, and education of service recipients?	3	–2
Do we invest in staff training in how to design and print our own marketing materials?	4	0
Total of Column Score (Add up each column and put the answer here.) ➜		
TOTAL SCORE (Add total scores from Yes and No columns and put the answer here.) ➜		

FORM0306.DOC

Form 3-7 Technology & Marketing (Chapter 10)	Yes	No
Do we maintain e-mail lists of our donors, contacts, supporters, funders, etc?	3	−1
Do we design, edit, amend, update, and print our own marketing materials?	3	0
Do we give staff who need phones/pagers the tools to stay in touch?	3	−3
Do we regularly compare our web site's content, look, and ease of use with our peer organizations?	2	−1
Do we have an online newsletter?	2	0
Does our web site have the ability to accept donations?	4	−3
Do potential volunteers have a way to contact us through our web site?	1	−1
Do we have the ability to survey (and collate the data) online?	1	−1
Do we have a live person answering the phone during business hours? Do callers reach this person first, before getting a recording?	3	−5
Do we have voice mail for staff?	3	−1
Total of Column Score (Add up each column and put the answer here.) ➜		
TOTAL SCORE (Add total scores from Yes and No columns and put the answer here.) ➜		

FORM0307.DOC

Form 3-8   Incredible Customer Service (Chapter 11)

	Yes	No
Do all of our staff get at least two hours of customer service training annually?	3	−2
Do we train our staff to have a sense of compassionate urgency about everyone we serve?	3	0
Do our staff understand that everyone is a customer, including our funders?	2	−2
Do we tell our staff that while customers may not always be right, they are customers, so fix the problem and fix it now?	2	−1
Do we empower them to fix these problems?	3	−2
Do we focus on customer satisfaction as opposed to customer service?	2	0
Total of Column Score (Add up each column and put the answer here.) ➜		
TOTAL SCORE (Add total scores from Yes and No columns and put the answer here.) ➜		

● FORM0308.DOC

Form 3-9 Marketing Planning (Chapter 12)

	Yes	No
Do we have a current marketing plan (three to five years)?	3	−1
Are both board *and* staff involved in the marketing planning process?	2	−1
Do we float drafts of our plan widely both inside and outside the organization?	3	−1
Does our planning process include the people we serve, the funding sources, and the community?	2	−1
Do we regularly review progress at implementing the marketing plan at staff and board meetings?	2	0
Are our marketing goals and objectives part of our strategic plan?	2	0
Does our marketing plan delineate our target markets, our core competencies, and how we plan to meet our markets' wants?	3	−2
Total of Column Score (Add up each column and put the answer here.) →		
TOTAL SCORE (Add total scores from Yes and No columns and put the answer here.) →		

FORM0309.DOC

Form 3-10 Self-Assessment Score Compilation

Instructions: Review your earlier scoring. Transfer the score for each area, and then sum your total self-assessment score at the bottom of the form.

Area	Your Score	Possible Score
Flexibility		13
The Marketing Cycle		22
Your Markets		21
Your Competition		16
Asking Your Markets		16
Your Marketing Materials		32
Technology & Marketing		25
Incredible Customer Service		15
Marketing Planning		17
Total Self-Assessment Score		177

 FORM0310.DOC

Remember, this is just an *initial* assessment. One of its uses is to get your collective organizational consciousness up and running in relation to marketing, as well as to give you a heads-up about what will be coming in future chapters of the book and the workbook. You will use the remainder of the workbook to go into more detail in each area, and I have included suggestions and checklists for each topic to help you improve your score, and your overall ability to be market driven and still mission based. Keep a copy of this score, and when you are done with the workbook, come back and do the self-assessment again. I'm sure you will see big improvements.

C. FORMS ON THE COMPANION CD-ROM

Form 3-11   Forms on the Companion CD-ROM

Form Name	Form No.	Workbook Page	File Name	File Format
Self-Assessment— Flexibility	3-1	13	FORM0301.DOC	Word for Windows
Self-Assessment— The Marketing Cycle	3-2	14	FORM0302.DOC	Word for Windows
Self-Assessment— Market Identification	3-3	15	FORM0303.DOC	Word for Windows
Self-Assessment— Your Competition	3-4	16	FORM0304.DOC	Word for Windows
Self-Assessment— Asking Your Markets	3-5	17	FORM0305.DOC	Word for Windows
Self-Assessment— Your Marketing Materials	3-6	18	FORM0306.DOC	Word for Windows
Self-Assessment— Technology & Marketing	3-7	19	FORM0307.DOC	Word for Windows
Self-Assessment— Incredible Customer Service	3-8	20	FORM0308.DOC	Word for Windows
Self-Assessment— Marketing Planning	3-9	21	FORM0309.DOC	Word for Windows
Self-Assessment— Scoring Compilation	3-10	22	FORM0310.DOC	Word for Windows
Forms on the Companion CD-ROM	3-11	23	FORM0311.DOC	Word for Windows

⏺ FORM0311.DOC

D. RESOURCES FOR FURTHER STUDY

Topic: Self-Assessment/General Management

Books

The Drucker Foundation Self-Assessment Tool: Process Guide by Peter Drucker, Gary Stern, and Francis Hesselbien. Jossey-Bass, 1998. (ISBN 078794436X).

Evaluation with Power: Developing Organization Effectiveness by Sandra Trice Gray. Jossey-Bass, 1997. (ISBN 0787909130).

Reengineering Your Nonprofit Organization: A Guide to Strategic Transformation by Alceste T. Pappas. John Wiley & Sons, 1995. (ISBN 0471118079).

All of these are periodicals about the not-for-profit sector and have some segment in each issue about marketing or development. You can view them and subscribe to them at the following URLS:

www.nptimes.com

www.boardcafe.org

www.philanthropy.com

You can also subscribe to my free monthly e-newsletter that includes a marketing tip each issue. Send an e-mail to *subscribe@missionbased.com*.

Software

None that I am aware of, but keep checking.

Web Sites

Andy Lewis' detailed self-assessment for nonprofits, based on the Learning Institute's eight-part organizational course, includes some material by me:
www.uwex.edu/li/learner/assessment.htm

Online self-assessment tool: originally designed for housing but with lots of applications for most not-for-profits:
www.ruralhome.org/pubs/workbooks/saworkbook/contents.htm

The nonprofit FAQ section on self-assessment—pretty good:
www.nonprofits.org/npofaq/03/26.html

Free management library—an incredibly deep and wide resource, I have highlighted just the link on marketing, but make sure to look around when you are there:
www.mapnp.org/library/mrktng/mrktng.htm

Free management site on outcome-based evaluation:
www.mapnp.org/library/evaluatn/outcomes.htm

Topic: Self-Assessment/General Management *(continued)*

This site has a ton of great stuff about marketing, including some current book, course, and tape listings:
http://nonprofitexpert.com/marketing.htm

Online Courses

Nonprofit Self-Grassroots MBA This online set of classes is designed for you to take at your own speed, and it covers all kinds of management skills, including marketing:
www.mapnp.org/library/mgmnt/mba_prog.htm

Nonprofit Education: This site is the most complete for nonprofit academic programs all over North America. Check out the institutions to find the most up-to-date online offerings, which are increasing every month:
http://pirate.shu.edu/~mirabero/Kellogg.html

4

Organizational Flexibility

A. STRAIGHT FROM *MISSION-BASED MARKETING*

Here's the key material from Chapter 4 in *Mission-Based Marketing*. My point is to remind you and your marketing team that in order to meet the ever-changing wants of many different markets, you need to remain flexible—both individually and organizationally.

A crucial point (and secret) about change:

> *It's the steady change, the small improvements every day, not the huge makeovers, that make the difference. Not only are they more effective, but they are also easier for staff and board to accommodate.*

Put another way:

> *Incremental change is less painful. Less pain means less resistance.*

Why is this statement true? Because if you are market driven, if you are asking, listening, asking and listening in relentless persistence, then you will hear about 1000 small ways in which you can make your customers happier for every one major change. If you change 1 percent a day, in just 100 days (or one third of a year), the entire organization is renewed—but at a pace to which your staff can adjust and adapt. Steady change is the secret.

All of us are born flexible. As we age, we all lose our flexibility. I'm sure that you have watched toddlers bend in ways that would put you or me in the hospital. As we get older, we have to work hard on flexibility or it disappears (much to our disadvantage).

Mentally, we can become inflexible as well. By not continuing to learn, or not continuing to consider new ideas or new ways of doing work, our mental processes get set in a rut just as surely as our muscles, tendons, and joints do. When you hear yourself saying (or thinking), "Ah, that new stuff doesn't interest me. We're doing just fine," alarms should go off. Sometimes the "new stuff" *is* questionable, but more often there is progress to be embraced. Even if an entire new idea, process, or protocol is not completely applicable to your organization, some of it might be. Thus, regular study and reading to both stretch your brain and learn something that might be of value to you later is important. Fight mental rigidity.

Organizationally, we become inflexible as well. We get invested in our buildings—a syndrome that I call the "edifice complex." This complex results from having so much of our assets invested in our building that the building *becomes* the organization. We become product-oriented, and the product is what we do in the building. If we have classrooms, inpatient beds, display space, or even offices, we *have* to fill them—whether or not the market wants what goes into those spaces.

"The hurrieder I go, the behinder I get" is an old saying that speaks well to the feeling we all have at times about the world in which we live. No one can possibly keep up with the changes in their profession or workplace, in fashion, sports, music, technology, entertainment, politics, and local, national, and international events. So, we have a tendency to throw up our hands and say "Overload!" and find excuses not to pay attention.

In the "old" days, you could get away with that for a number of reasons. Change was slower paced; you got a break from people if you weren't "cutting edge" because you were a not-for-profit, and most importantly, you probably had a relative or virtual monopoly. Thus, it didn't matter how much you accommodated changes in the "outside" world. You could accommodate at your own more leisurely (and more professional) pace. Remember when attorneys and physicians berated those in their professions who advertised? Now, you go down the road and see huge billboards advertising for law practices, medical groups, clinics, hospitals, and even individual practitioners. And some of those who refused to advertise are out of business or have been bought out by their competition.

There are two key points I want to make here, and they are both contained in the header at the beginning of this chapter. First, there is the *pace of change*. It is accelerating with the explosion of information available, the speed of communications, and the general pace of our lives all being more and more intense. Second, there is the *competitive environment*. This environment is one that your organization might already be in or might just be entering. But you and your organization cannot avoid it. Imagine you are at a huge airport. You are walking down an immense concourse to your plane. Suddenly, you come up on a moving walkway and are forced by the crowd to get on. Your pace has just picked up. Now, the walkway speeds up ever so steadily until you are nearly racing. Things go by faster. You have less time to study them before they are behind you. The end of the walkway comes up very, very fast. That is the transition from non-competitive to competitive environments and from the slower pace of yesteryear to the rapid pace of today.

B. BASELINE SELF-ASSESSMENT

Note: the self-assessment in Form 4–1 includes the questions you answered in Chapter 3 plus a number of new ones. Go through and score your organization as best you can. Do this assessment as a group, if possible, or individually, and then collate your scores.

Form 4-1 Flexibility Self-Assessment

	Yes	No
Are we doing just the same services in the same way as three years ago?	2	−2
Is change considered an opportunity to improve as opposed to a threat to the status quo?	3	−1
Did we make money in each of the past three years as an organization?	3	−1
Is at least 5 percent of our income unrestricted?	2	−1
Are we concerned about regular small improvements in services?	3	0
Do we ask customers (of all kinds, internal, external, funder, and service) regularly for ideas on how to improve our services to them?	2	−1
Do we listen and seriously consider those ideas?	4	−2
Do we value and encourage risk taking?	3	−2
Do we publicly equate changes in service to mission improvement?	2	−1
When we make a change, do we avoid criticizing the past?	2	0
Total of Column Score (Add up each column and put the answer here.) ➜		
TOTAL SCORE—FLEXIBILITY (Add total scores from Yes and No columns and put the answer here.) ➜		

● FORM0401.DOC

SCORING ANALYSIS:

20–26 Excellent
14–19 Very Good
12–18 Adequate
Less than 12—You need to look further at your organizational flexibility.

As you look at your flexibility, remember that the idea is to be open to change but not to knee-jerk to every market whim. Use your mission statement and your values to keep you on the right track.

C. WORKSHEETS AND CHECKLISTS

Form 4-2 details some things you can do to improve your flexibility.

Form 4-2 **Flexibility Checklist**		
Y		**Review your flexibility. Ask these questions:**
		How can we encourage more flexibility?
		Do we encourage risk taking in pursuit of mission? How? How can we do more?
		How can we become more financially flexible? Can we increase our net unrestricted income? Do we have adequate cash on hand and access to cash?
		How does our board feel about change, risk, and flexibility?
		Do we have barriers externally to flexibility (such as funder rules and regulations)? What are they? How can we start to address them now?
		Specifically how have we changed in the past three years? (See the first **HANDS-ON** below for ideas.) Can we list the changes to illustrate the fact that as an organization we are moving forward?
		Do we truly listen to our customers when they suggest improvements and changes? How can we be better at this?
Y		Ask the staff how the organization can improve its listening skills for all its markets. Also seek ideas on how to become internally more flexible.
Y		Meet with the board and staff, discuss your findings. Talk about necessary changes.
Y		The mission statement should be evident everywhere: On the wall, marketing materials, the back of staff business cards, screen savers, on the annual report, and the table at board and staff meetings. This will keep you from simply reacting to any and all market changes. It will help keep you true to your mission.

● FORM0402.DOC

Form 4-3 can be used to write down the things you need to do from the checklist in Form 4-2.

Form 4-3 **Implementation Checklist** **Topic: Flexibility**		
Measurable Outcome	**Deadline**	**Person or Group Responsible**

● FORM0403.DOC

D. ☞ HANDS-ON

Here are the ☞ HANDS-ON ideas from Chapter 4 of *Mission-Based Marketing:*

☞ HANDS-ON: To emphasize how many changes you have made in your organization in the recent past, do this exercise with your staff and/or board members. Look at your organization five years ago. If you have pictures, policies, staff lists, board lists, marketing material, audits, and annual reports, use them to make a comparison of then versus now. Specifically, look at:

• *Size*. How much income do you have per year now versus five years ago?

• *Programs*. Do you have more programs? Are the ones that you have now provided differently than then? How?

• *Location*. Have you moved? Have you purchased or sold a building?

- *Staff.* How many new people have been added to the staff? How many of those on staff five years ago have left?

- *Board.* What changes in the board have you seen?

- *Policies.* How have your personnel, financial, quality assurance, and bylaws changed?

- *Funders.* What is your funding mix? Do you get funding from different sources than five years ago? What changes in reporting and accounting have you noticed? In auditing and oversight have there been changes?

- *Technology.* Do you use the same computers and software as five years ago? Cell phones? Faxes? Internet provider? How much has your web site changed? Did you have your own organizational URL two years ago? Five years ago?

As you answer these questions as a group, you will see that you have changed **a lot.** Talk about these changes. Some were easy, and some were painful. But reinforce the fact that your organization has *successfully* changed in many ways and that you can continue to do it in the future.

☞ **HANDS-ON:** Take out your most recent balance sheet and a calculator. Look at your fixed assets, and divide them by your total assets. Are fixed assets more than 75 percent of all your assets? Now, look at your cash and cash equivalents. Does it equal or exceed more than 60 days' operation? If you have too many fixed assets and too little cash, you are hamstrung when it comes to quickly accommodating changes in the market.

☞ **HANDS-ON:** Try these changes:

Low Impact

- *Change your letterhead.* You do not have to change it now, but do it when your supply runs out. I'm not talking about changing the logo or the entire look (which might be timely as well) but rather moving the lines, changing the color, and so on. I know that this task might require a change in business cards, and so on, but those can be phased in over time.

- *Repaint, re-paper, put down new carpet.* Don't ever think that a change of appearance is unimportant. If you have the money, give staff an allowance to buy wall decorations for their offices.

- *Upgrade your software.* Most software has regular upgrades, and many are available online to download. If yours are functional but not completely up-to-date, consider upgrading. It is often not expensive, sometimes even free, and you can be more productive after the change.

- *Rethink your meeting schedules.* Do you need staff meetings every week or team meetings every month? Are the location, duration, and content of the meetings appropriate? Ask those who regularly attend, and make the changes that they suggest.

- *Start with your own environment.* Move your own office furniture, add a plant, or remove a picture. Buy a new coffee mug, eat lunch at a different time each day, or drive a new route to work. As I wrote the second edition of this book, I moved my office furniture around for—I admit it—the first time in five years. The positive change in my attitude upon arriving at my office every day (and I *like* coming to work) was amazing, and I resolved to move things about more often. Get used to difference, adapting, and change, and lead your people as you do.

High Impact

- *Change offices.* Whoa—here is a big one. Perhaps a change of location will help some people or be an avenue for better communication, more effective supervision, or improved access to your clientele.

- *Change titles.* Starting with your own. Perhaps you have been thinking of moving to a corporate model where the executive director has the title of CEO and where people who were directors become vice-presidents. Perhaps now is the time to implement that.

- *Reorganize your table of organization.* Not just to do it, but if you have been putting a needed change off, get on with it. Perhaps there will be a major reorganization, or perhaps just a few people will be affected.

- *Change your committee makeup.* On the staff level, this task is pretty easy. I have always encouraged organizations to have representation on their committees from all levels of the organization, both vertically and horizontally. In other words, make changes from all levels of management and from all parts of the organization. If you haven't done that, start now. If you have, shuffle some staff from one committee to another (asking them first, of course, if they have any preference). At the board level, talk to your board president about implementing a needed new committee, or changing the job descriptions on existing ones, moving board members around, or even changing the staff who are responsible for particular committees.

E. FORMS ON THE COMPANION CD-ROM

Form 4-4   Forms on the Companion CD-ROM

Form Name	Form No.	Workbook Page	File Name	File Format
Flexibilty Self-Assessment	4-1	28	FORM0401.DOC	Word for Windows
Flexiblity Checklist	4-2	29	FORM0402.DOC	Word for Windows
Implementation Checklist	4-3	30	FORM0403.DOC	Word for Windows
Forms on the Companion CD-ROM	4-4	33	FORM0404.DOC	Word for Windows

FORM0404.DOC

F. RESOURCES FOR FURTHER STUDY

Topic: Flexibility
Books
Change-ABLE Organization: Key Management Practices for Speed & Flexibility by William R. Daniels and John G. Mathers. ACT Publishing, 1997.
Software
None that I am aware of here, but keep checking.
Web Sites
The Free Management Library on Change: *www.mapnp.org/library/org_chng/org_chng.htm*
Online Courses
Nonprofit Self-Grassroots MBA—This online set of classes is designed for you to take at your own speed, and it covers all kinds of management skills, including marketing: *www.mapnp.org/library/mgmnt/mba_prog.htm*

5

The Marketing Cycle

A. STRAIGHT FROM *MISSION-BASED MARKETING*

The marketing cycle is really a way to continuously improve your services and products. If you follow the ideas here from *Mission-Based Marketing,* you will have a great deal of success in becoming a market-driven and still mission-based organization.

The Marketing Cycle That Works

Most people seem to think that the marketing cycle starts with the product or service. If I know what I am selling, the theory seems to go, then I start from that point. I then can decide how to sell, who to sell to, what way to convince them, and how to price. As noted in the introduction to this chapter, that sentiment is wrong, wrong, wrong, and wrong again. Marketing doesn't start with the product or the service. Marketing starts with the *market:* the people to whom you are trying to sell or to serve. If you start by deciding who you are serving, follow that by asking those people what they want and then respond by giving it to them, that's marketing. If you start with a product or service and back into a market by asking, "How can I sell this wonderful product or service to these people?", you are destined to succeed only for a short time and then only if you are a superb salesperson.

Marketing (the verb) has to start with the market (the noun) to be effective over the long haul. And, by putting the appropriate marketing activities together in the correct sequence, you can change the way your organization thinks of its markets and ultimately the way those markets think of you (hopefully for the better). The cycle that we're about to review works for new products and new services and for honing and improving existing products or services. It works in human services, the arts, education, religion, environmental action, and legal aid. It works because at its core it is sensitive to people's wants, not their needs, and it puts those wants first.

With no further delay, let's review this marketing cycle. Exhibit 5-1 shows the cycle at its purest and simplest, in a generic form that can be used across disciplines.

Exhibit 5-1   **The Marketing Cycle**

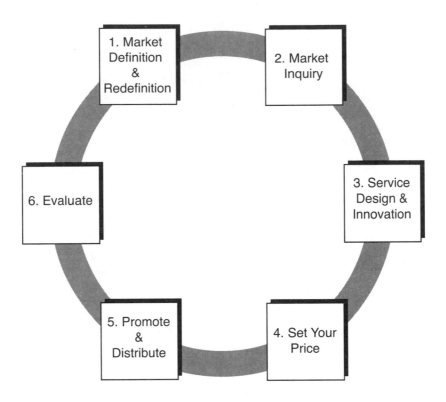

As you can see, the cycle starts with the identification of the target markets, works its way through asking about the markets' wants, and then designs or modifies the product or service that you are going to provide. Nowhere in the display do you see the word "need." There's a reason for that, and you should know the answer if you read Chapter 2: needs are different than wants, and wants are what people buy, not needs.

Let's dissect the cycle and go through it item by item, discussing each point in some detail. Then, we'll reassemble the cycle and look at its application in some real-world not-for-profits.

- *Market Definition & Redefinition.* This phase sounds so basic that it creeps up on people (see Exhibit 5-2). But the first question to ask is, "Who am I serving?" Who are the people, the individuals to whom I am selling? How many of them are there? Where are they? Are they as a group, as a market, growing in numbers or waning? As you approach this question, do not get sucked up into "the census trap." You get caught in the census trap when you assume that your market is all the people in a geographic area. It never is. This assumption is an outgrowth of the monopolies that we discussed at length in Chapter 1. Many organizations had (and some still have) cachement areas (areas that were their "territory," or their monopoly). In many cases, funding for these organizations was based on population (capitated) so that the illusion that an organization worked for everyone in the cachement area was reinforced.

Nothing, of course, could be farther from the truth. Your market is not everyone; it is a much, much more defined group of people. If you are a private school, your market is the parents of children in the age groups you teach who are interested in non-public education and who have the resources to send their children to your school. If you are a health department, for health screenings your market might be just people who don't have private physicians. Or, if it were lead screenings, your market could be people with very small children who lived in older homes with lead-based paint. If you are a church, while your dogma might suggest that the world is your market, in reality you are most likely going to appeal to people within 5-8 miles of your church who are looking for a church and who do not already have a church home. A much smaller number than "everyone" in the community or even within your 5-8 mile radius.

Exhibit 5-2 Market Definition

```
┌─────────────────────┐
│                     │
│   1. Market         │
│   Definition        │
│   &                 │
│   Redefinition      │
│                     │
└─────────────────────┘
```

The action statement in italics says "Market Definition & Redefinition." Defining a market is pretty straightforward: you identify who you are going to serve. But what do I mean by redefining? It is an important term, because for most readers it will be the more common task. Redefining your market(s) means to periodically go back and look at your markets, assure that they are still there, ensure that they are the ones you want to serve and verify that they still have wants that you can meet. For example, if you are a YMCA and one of your markets (for your athletic summer camps) is kids from ages 8-18, you might re-examine this market and redefine it to be *kids ages 8-18 from homes that have incomes over $30,000* or *kids from public schools* as opposed to private schools, or *kids who played in your regular youth athletic leagues*. This regular redefinition is crucial because conditions change, markets mature, and wants change along with them. Only by regularly reviewing and redefining who it is that you are serving can you accurately ask those whom you hope to serve what they want.

I hope that you get the idea that you need to identify your target markets carefully, developing as detailed a definition and as particular a description of them as you can. The more accurate and finite your definition of your market, the more accurate your market projections will be (and thus your estimates, assumptions, and plans). This technique should be used for all of your services, for all of your markets, so that you can recognize the many different markets that you serve. This activity is so important that we will spend the entirety of Chapter 6 solely on this subject.

- *Market Inquiry (Or What Do Your Markets Really Want?).* Having identified your market(s) as closely and finitely as you can, what is next? Is it to figure out how to sell your product or service to this newly identified group? Is it to blanket them with literature so that they will want what you have to sell? Is it to offer coupons to entice them into your doors the first time? No, not yet.

Exhibit 5-3 **What Does the Market Want?**

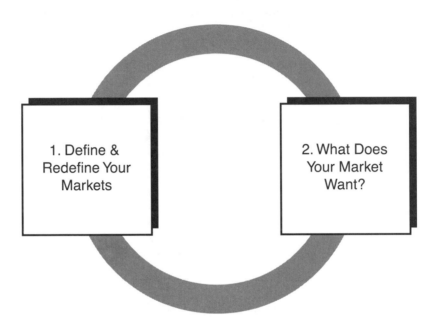

What is next in the marketing cycle is to figure out what the market wants (see Exhibit 5-3). How do you do that, you ask? By doing just that: *asking.* By asking regularly and then, of course, *listening* and *responding,* you will find out what most people want. Remember our discussion in Chapter 2—people seek wants, so meet those wants and people will seek out your organization.

You can ask formally or informally. You can ask in surveys, in focus groups, in interviews, or in one-on-one conversation. You can ask in person or online. However you do it, you need to ask and ask again. Asking once is not enough, because people's wants change and change regularly. This issue is also critical, and we'll spend the entirety of Chapter 8 asking in all of its ways.

Suffice it to say that you cannot meet your markets' wants if you don't know what those wants are. And, you cannot know what the wants are unless you ask. The biggest mistake that you can make in marketing is to say, "I've been in this business 20 years and I *know* what customers want." Wrong. No one knows until they ask. Ask, ask, ask, and listen.

• *Service Design & Innovation*. Only now that you know who your target market is and only now that you know what they want, can you shape (or reshape) your product or service to meet the wants of your target market (see Exhibit 5-4). This may mean starting from scratch to develop a new product or service, or more likely the constant amendment, innovation in, and improvement of products and services already in place. Remember, not only will you be redefining your markets regularly, but wants change with time. Even within static markets, wants change. As a result, you need to assess and reassess and reassess your services to assure that they meet the current wants of the markets.

Exhibit 5-4   Meeting the Needs of the Market

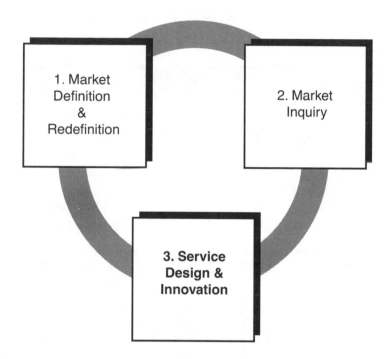

You cannot reasonably meet *every* want of *every* market. For example, if one potential customer for counseling services says that he or she can only come in between midnight and eight in the morning, it is probably not reasonable or cost-efficient to have a counselor on site overnight just for one customer. The information is important, however, because it might point out a previously hidden market—those who work second-shift jobs and are ready to seek services at night rather than during traditional hours. Is there enough of a market to support a reshaping of your services to accommodate this want?

You need to be sensitive to regular changes in market wants by making adjustments in the way you provide your services. You need to cushion your desire to meet every customer's need fully with prudent business assessments and financial planning, however, to assure that you meet the wants you can afford to and defer on those that you cannot do either efficiently, effectively, or with a high degree of quality.

- *Set Your Price*. A sensible price is one that recovers all of your costs of providing a service or manufacturing a product, adds a profit to that price, and, meets the realities of the market (see Exhibit 5-5). The first and second parts increase the price. The third part usually reduces it.

Let me focus you for a moment on the first part: full cost recovery. I know far too many organizations that are convinced that they must underprice their competition at any cost; that cost is all that motivates a customer. Thus, they often juggle their costs around so that their sales price appears to be one that assures full cost recovery but really doesn't. In this way, they feel that they are assured of getting the work and of locking in the customer. What they are *really* doing is assuring that each time they provide the service they *lose* money.

Exhibit 5-5   Setting the Price

```
┌─────────────────┐                    ┌─────────────────┐
│ 1. Market       │                    │ 2. Market       │
│    Definition   │                    │    Inquiry      │
│    &            │                    │                 │
│    Redefinition │                    │                 │
└─────────────────┘                    └─────────────────┘


┌─────────────────┐                    ┌─────────────────┐
│ 4. Set Your     │                    │ 3. Service      │
│    Price        │                    │    Design &     │
│                 │                    │    Innovation   │
└─────────────────┘                    └─────────────────┘
```

It is crucial in price setting to remember that people don't buy based on price—they buy based on *value*. Price is a variable component of value. For some people, price is 99 percent of value; for others it is just a small amount. If price was the only issue, there would not be any luxury products or services, no first-class seats on airlines, no Ritz Carleton hotels, no limousines clogging up the streets in our big cities, and so on. If price were everything, we would send all of our correspondence by first-class mail. Federal Express would shut down in a day. So would Gucci, Saks, and most of the stores on Fifth Avenue in New York or Rodeo Drive in Beverly Hills.

So, don't just think about price. Think about value. And never tell people what they should value—that's giving them what they *need*. Ask them what they value, and then give them what they *want*. Do people highly value your service or the way that you deliver it?

If so, they will be willing to consider paying more for it. If they don't value your services, then even a lower price might not bring them on as a customer.

Don't ever assume that price is everything. Recover your costs, add a profit, and then listen to the markets. This issue is also really important, and I have included a complete chapter on the subject in my book *Financial Empowerment* (Brinckerhoff, John Wiley & Sons, 1998).

- *Promote & Distribute?* By now your know your market, you know what it wants, you know what you are providing, and you know the price. Great. But does your market know about you? Do they know that you are in business and that you have this wonderful product or service that is shaped to meet their wants? This area is called advertising. It is cold calls, warm calls, direct mail, word of mouth, in-person sales, referrals, and public information. Don't just shotgun your information. Carefully gauge how and what you tell your markets. Track how they find you, and use only those methods that work. Experiment with new ones, but drop them if they are not delivering for you. A great example of this trial and error is the explosion in web sites on the Internet that has occurred since 1995. Have they resulted in more business? For some organizations, yes; for some, no. The net offers access to huge markets, but are they the people you want to seek? Many of my clients have come to the conclusion that they must have a web site because it is a cost of doing business and that the most mission that they can do on the site is good public information and education.

Exhibit 5-6 Promotion and Distribution

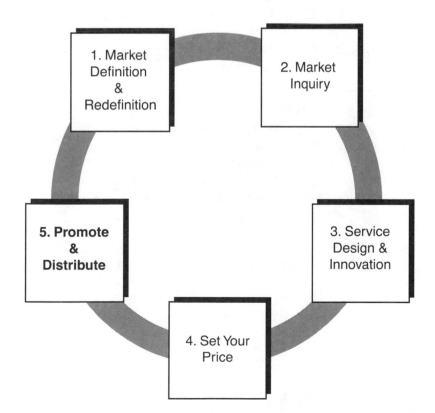

You need to promote to customers, to people who you serve, and to people who send you customers (your referral sources). For a rehabilitation hospital, these sources might be neurologists; for an ex-offender program, it might be court adjudicators; or for a wildlife preserve it might be travel agents or local hotels and restaurants. You need referral sources, and you need to give them information that helps them understand what you do and why they should send people to you.

Here again is a very important issue. You need excellent marketing materials, and you need to put them in the right hands at the right time. So, better marketing materials will be our entire focus in Chapter 9.

Distribution is a common marketing term, but it might be easier for you to think of it as service delivery with the following context: who, when, where, and how. Remember that all of these context items weigh heavily on market satisfaction. A simple example is daycare. If the *who* is not people who relate well to children (and parents); if the *when* is not at hours that meet parents' work schedules; if the *where* is not in an accessible location perceived as open, airy, pleasing, and safe; and if the *how* is not beneficial to the children, then the services will not be patronized well enough to do the community any good.

By asking your customers what they want, you will learn a great deal about how they want the services provided. This cycle of asking and providing is yet another case of constant refinement. If there is a change in the wants for delivery, try to meet it if you can sensibly. For example, to use the daycare example, if your community's largest employer (a factory) suddenly went to a second or even a third shift, you might need to rethink the hours that you provide services. But if only one or two families out of 100 need the extended hours, you might offer them in-home sitting rather than keeping the entire facility open all night.

Just because the *what* of your services is excellent doesn't mean that you don't have to pay attention to the *who, where, when,* and *how*. They are also part of the marketing mix and the constant cycle of asking and adjustment.

- *Evaluate, Evaluate, Evaluate.* As you have already seen repeatedly, the markets and their wants change constantly. You need to be evaluating the effectiveness of your efforts, as well. Customer satisfaction surveys are one way, as are regular interviews with funders, service recipients, and staff and board members. But you also need to be watching competitors and tracking where your customers come from. All of these evaluation tools are important. In later chapters, we'll cover how to choose and segment markets, follow the competition, and ask customers what they want, but the essential thing here is to remember that evaluation and improvement are critical parts of the competitive marketing cycle.

You can see that once you evaluate, you start over again—and, as I said earlier, the marketing cycle doesn't ever end, it just keeps going, helping you focus more resources on markets that want them.

Exhibit 5-7 Completing the Cycle

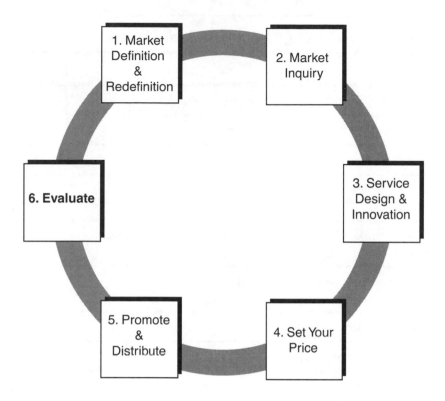

B. BASELINE SELF-ASSESSMENT

Form 5-1 The Marketing Cycle Self-Assessment	Yes	No
Do we identify our markets before we figure out what they want?	3	–3
Do we know our three key (target) payer markets?	3	0
Do we know our three key (target) service markets?	3	0
Do we consider how we provide services in light of what these markets want?	3	–1
Do we promote our services and products to meet wants as opposed to needs?	2	–1
Are we stuck in a *needs assessment* only mode, or do we really consider what our service recipients *want?*	3	–3
Do we review the prices we can control every six months?	2	0
Do we have an evaluation component to our marketing effort?	3	0
Do we reevaluate our markets annually?	4	0
Do we know our core competencies?	3	0
Do we try to match those competencies against the wants of our target markets?	2	0
Do we price to make money when we can?	2	–2
Do we look at expenditures as investments in mission?	3	–1
Do we evaluate how people hear about us, so that we can promote where they are listening?	3	–2
Do we provide services in ways we know people want?	3	–1
Total of Column Score (Add up each column and put the answer here.) ➡		
TOTAL SCORE—BOARD OF DIRECTORS (Add total scores from Yes and No columns and put the answer here.) ➡		

FORM0501.DOC

SCORING ANALYSIS:
36–42 Excellent
27–35 Very Good
16–26 Adequate
Less than 16—You need to work on the items listed here. Understanding the marketing cycle is crucial.

As you begin the process of improving your organization, you will find many of the questions listed in the self-assessment in the following chapters, as well. That is due to the fact that so many of the issues raised in the marketing cycle have corollary issues in the specialty chapters of the workbook. But do not put off addressing the items in the assessment.

C. WORKSHEETS AND CHECKLISTS

Form 5-2 **Marketing Cycle Checklist**	
Y	Do we know who our markets are?
	Have we identified all of our markets?
	Have we identified our three target payer markets?
	Have we identified our three target service markets?
	Do we know who our three most important referral sources are?
Y	Do we have a plan to regularly ask our markets what they want?
Y	Once we know what our markets want, do we have a formal process to listen to those wants and regularly improve services and products?
Y	Do we have a process for regularly reviewing the prices that we can control?
Y	Do we know where people hear about us? Do we target our promotion in those areas?

● FORM0502.DOC

Fill in this sheet looking at your markets, and then fill in what you think they want.

Form 5-3 **Who Are Our Markets?**		
Markets	**Wants**	**How Do We Know What They Want?**
Payer Markets		
Service Markets		
Referral Markets		

FORM0503.DOC

Use Form 5-4 to write down the things you need to do from the previous checklist, or to list other key issues to resolve.

Form 5-4 **Implementation Checklist** **Topic: The Marketing Cycle**		
Measurable Outcome	**Deadline**	**Person or Group Responsible**

● FORM0504.DOC

D. ☞ HANDS-ON

☞ **HANDS-ON:** Talk to your staff, particularly your highest-trained staff, about the importance of listening to the wants of the people you serve. Remind them that listening is not an inherited skill; rather, it is a practiced one, and listening (really listening) is not just waiting their turn to talk. Finally, work with them on how to see things from their customers', their clients', and their students' perspectives. The more that they can do that, the more value they will attach to the opinions, the complaints, the concerns, and *the wants* of the people who your organization serves.

☞ **HANDS-ON:** Sit down with your senior staff and ask them these questions: "What do we do better than our main competition?" "Can we do more?" "How do we know we are better?" "Can we improve on our best?" The idea is to reduce the fear of your competitors. As I have said over and over, you have competition. Are you doing something for someone that your competition can do as well or better? Then watch out, because they are watching you. You might need to redefine your market to accommodate to the competition.

☞ **HANDS-ON:** Get a copy of every one of your marketing and promotional pieces. Look at each one and write down whether it is a broad-based piece or a piece that is targeted to a particular market. If you have more broad-based than targeted pieces, you could be in real trouble if your competition is focused on one small (and usually lucrative) market.

E. FORMS ON THE COMPANION CD-ROM

Form 5-5 **Forms on the Companion CD-ROM**				
Form Name	**Form No.**	**Workbook Page**	**File Name**	**File Format**
Marketing Cycle Self-Assessment	5-1	44	FORM0501.DOC	Word for Windows
Marketing Cycle Checklist	5-2	45	FORM0502.DOC	Word for Windows
Market Identification	5-3	46	FORM0503.DOC	Word for Windows
Implementation Checklist	5-4	47	FORM0504.DOC	Word for Windows
Forms on the Companion CD-ROM	5-5	48	FORM0505.DOC	Word for Windows

● FORM0505.DOC

F. RESOURCES FOR FURTHER STUDY

Topic: The Marketing Cycle

Publications and Periodicals

Strategic Communications for Nonprofit Organizations: Seven Steps to Creating a Successful Plan (Nonprofit Law, Finance, and Management Series) by Janel M. Radtke. John Wiley & Sons, 1998. (ISBN 0471174645).

Successful Marketing Strategies for Nonprofit Organizations (Nonprofit Law, Finance, and Management) by Barry L. McLeish. John Wiley & Sons, August 1995. (ISBN 0471105678).

Marketing Workbook for Nonprofit Organizations: Develop the Plan, 2nd edition, by Gary J. Stern, Elana Centor, Vol 1, March 2001. Amherst H. Wilder Foundation. (ISBN 0940069253).

Software

Market Plan Pro: This program is really marketing planning software, but it asks all the right questions. You can also see a ton of marketing plans at *www.paloalto.com.*

Web Sites

www.nonprofitmarketing.org

The Free Management Library's take on marketing:
www.mapnp.org/library/mrktng/mrktng.htm

Online Courses

Nonprofit Self-Grassroots MBA This online set of classes is designed for you to take at your own speed, and it covers all kinds of management skills, including marketing: *www.mapnp.org/library/mgmnt/mba_prog.htm*

Nonprofit Education: This site is the most complete site for nonprofit academic programs all over North America. Check out the institutions to find the most up-to-date online offerings, which increase every month: *http://pirate.shu.edu/~mirabero/Kellogg.html*

6

Who Are Your Markets?

A. STRAIGHT FROM *MISSION-BASED MARKETING*

The first step in the marketing cycle we looked at in Chapter 5 was defining your markets. We did a bit of that in the last chapter, but now we need to really focus on market definition and segmentation. Here are some things to remember from *Mission-Based Marketing*.

Market Indentification and Quantification

So, who are these markets to which we keep referring? Let's look at a diagram that will help you focus on the many, many different markets you actually serve. As you look at Exhibit 6-1, note how many markets there are and keep in mind that this diagram probably does not include all of *your* organization's markets.

Exhibit 6-1   The Markets of a Not-for-Profit

Internal	• Board of Directors • Staff Members • Volunteers	
Payer	• Government • Membership • Foundations • United Way • Donations • Insurers • User Fees	

Service
(More than just the two shown as examples)
	• **Service A**
	  —Client Type 1
	  —Client Type 2
	  —Client Type 3
	  —Client Type 4
	• **Service B**
	  —Client Type 1
	  —Client Type 2
	  —Client Type 3
	  —Client Type 4	

Referral Sources	• Many different sources, all with different wants.	

When I first suggested that you examine your markets, you probably immediately thought of the different groups of people you help through your services. That's understandable but only a part of the whole picture. You *really* have, as you can see, four different main categories of markets: internal, payer, referral, and service and probably 10, 20, or even 40 different markets contained within those four categories. Each category is important; you can't provide services without money or without a staff or a board, and nearly all organizations depend on a significant percentage of their work from referrals. Each category bears further analysis.

1. Internal Markets

There are three of these: your board, your staff, and your non-governing volunteers. All three are crucial, and all three deserve to be treated like markets—utilizing the same marketing process that we discussed in Chapter 5. All three groups deserve to have their wants met to the extent that you can. Unfortunately, most not-for-profits either ignore this issue or drastically underestimate the importance of these markets. They treat their board as a necessary evil, their staff as a commodity, and their volunteers even worse. The management "knows" what the staff wants (more money), so they never ask. The management doesn't really care what the board wants as long as they come to meetings and don't ask too many questions. Volunteers are to be put in whatever position is most in need, not matched with their skills, oriented, or trained.

The downfall of these perceptions is that in a competitive world, you need excellent board members, and to get and keep them you need to treat them as a valuable resource. Likewise, you are going to need to attract and retain good staff, and it will be tough: you need good staff more than they need you. For many readers, their volunteers are a huge payroll savings and provide a network into the community that no other force can. And, in a competitive world, board members, volunteers, and staff have lots of choices of where to put in their hours. It doesn't have to be at your place.

2. Payer Markets

These are the people who send you money for the services you provide. You might be offended that I consider these people a market. After all, you are here to do good works. Money is just a vehicle (and an unseemly one at that). The people you really need to pay attention to are the people you serve, right? Partially. In the old days of having a monopoly, you could afford this situation, but no more. If in a competitive market you ignore the payers and the internal markets and direct your attentions solely to the people you serve, you are on a short road to oblivion. Remember, there are two primary rules of not-for-profits. Rule one is "Mission, mission, mission." Rule two is "No money, no mission." Ignore these at your peril.

As you can see, there are many payers, and we should examine their different wants. I do need to caution you here: do *not* accept my listing of wants as gospel. Go ask them yourself.

- Government

- Membership

- Foundations

- United Way

- Donations

- Insurers

- User fees

3. Service Markets

Just as in the payer markets, there are many service markets. These are the people who you serve, and they can be broken down by age, gender, education, income, zip code, ethnicity, or the program(s) that they utilize. Most of you probably have thought that these were the people who you worked for and that this market was who you were serving. It is, but the internal and payer markets are essential as well. As with the payer markets, it is crucial that you avoid lumping the people you serve together. The more discrete groups that you can identify, the more you can focus your asking and responding to them.

4. Referrers

We've already noted that your organization, like all others, has a limit on how much time and money you can spend on marketing. Wouldn't it be great to have people (who you don't pay) out there sending you members, clients, students, or parishioners. You can, and you might already. These are called referral sources. These might simply be informal recommendations from happy customers—someone who went to a play at your theater and was impressed or a parent who loves how his or her child is developing in your preschool. Or, they can be formal referrals from another professional, such as a surgeon referring a head trauma patient to a vocational rehabilitation facility or a rabbi referring a troubled member of her congregation to a psychologist or psychiatrist.

All of your markets—internal, payer, referral, and service—deserve attention. Paying close attention to so many diverse groups is not always easy, especially because your organization, like all others, has only so much money and staff time to throw at even this critical activity. So what do you do? There are two more steps to take control of all this marketing identification. The first is to learn about market segmenting, where you turn the tables and think through who you *want* to serve and compare that to who you currently serve. Then, you focus on your targets. I'll show you how to do both, and we'll start with segmenting.

B. BASELINE SELF-ASSESSMENT

Form 6-1 **Who Are Our Markets?**		
	Yes	**No**
Do we know who all of our funder markets are?	3	–1
Do we know who all of our referral markets are?	3	–1
Do we know who all of our service recipient markets are?	3	–1
Have we developed 2 to 5 target markets in each of the above three areas?	4	–2
Have we assigned a member of our marketing team to be the key liason/expert for each target market?	3	–1
Have we gathered baseline data on all of our internal and external markets?	2	–1
Do we regularly check to see how our target markets have changed?	3	–1
Have we taken a look at our core competencies in relation to our markets?	2	0
Have we tried to break down our target markets into segments that we can serve better?	2	0
Are there markets we are serving that other organizations can serve better?	–2	2
Are there other demographic or geographic markets that we should consider?	2	–2
Total of Column Score (Add up each column and put the answer here.) ➜		
TOTAL SCORE (Add total scores from Yes and No columns and put the answer here.) ➜		

● FORM0601.DOC

SCORING ANALYSIS:
22–27 Excellent
16–21 Very Good
12–15 Adequate
**Less than 12—You need to look in more detail at your markets and who they are.
You have to know who you are serving to be able to ask what it is that they want.**

C. WORKSHEETS AND CHECKLISTS

Because we are dealing with the first step in the marketing cycle, I have included overall marketing training needs in this chapter.

Form 6-2	Training Checklist—Marketing			
Y	Training Type	For Which Staff	Deadline	Responsible Person
	The Marketing Team	All staff—annually		
	Core competencies	Marketing Team		
	Pricing	All financial and sales staff		
	Better surveys	Marketing Team		
	Customer satisfaction	All staff annually		

FORM0602.DOC

Form 6-3 Marketing Checklist—Target Market Identification

Y	Activity	Rationale	Deadline	Responsible Person
	Identify all discrete markets: Internal, Payer, Service, and Referral.	This takes a while, you will be surpised how many you have.		
	Draft initial target markets.	Using the large list, use your best guesses to pick an initial list of target markets.		
	Identify target market wants.	Ask, and then use the next worksheet.		
	Identify internal core competencies.	What do you *really* do *really* well?		
	Match core competencies with target market wants.	Match one with the other, focusing on what you can do well that people want now. Or, do you need to ramp up your skills to meet a target market's wants?		
	Revise target market list as needed.	You may find out that your target group should be another one.		

FORM0603.DOC

Form 6-4   What Do Our Markets Really Want?

Category	Market	Wants
		(As you identify your markets, ask them what they want, and put the information here. Then match up wants with core competencies in the next chart. Note that your markets can have more than one important want.)
Internal	Board	
	Staff	
	Other Volunteers	
Payer		
Service		
Referral		

FORM0604.DOC

Form 6-5 **Our Core Competencies—Matching Up to Wants**

Our organizational core competencies are:	For this form, fill in your organizational core competencies, remembering to only put down the things that you are really, really good at. Then, fill in your top target markets and their wants, and see if your competencies match up. If they don't, you either need to ramp up your competencies or change your target markets.
1	
2	
3	
4	
5	
6	

	Target Market	The Market Want	Our Competency
1			
2			
3			
4			
5			

FORM0605.DOC

Form 6-6 Implementation Checklist Topic: Who Are Your Markets?		
Measurable Outcome	**Deadline**	**Person or Group Responsible**

FORM0606.DOC

D. ☞ HANDS-ON

☞ **HANDS-ON:** If your organization receives government income, consider this question carefully. When was the last time you asked your government project officer/funder, "How can I make your job easier?" Never? You are not alone, but that kind of question is essential to stabilize and improve relationships with all customers. When you read Chapter 11, "Incredible Customer Service," remember that it applies to this market as well.

☞ **HANDS-ON:** As you make lists of your markets and their segments, ask yourself "Why are we providing this service?" and "Why are we serving this population?" If your immediate answer is solely "Because we always have," you should stop and assess whether or not you should continue. Think through issues such as, do you have true expertise in the service or population? Is the service provided elsewhere as (or more) efficiently? Is this a core constituency for your organization? Is your organization identified primarily with this program or service population? Would reducing or ending this service dramatically affect your fundraising? And, of course, a crucial but not stand-alone indicator is, "Are you making or losing money in this area or with this group?" Answers to these and many other questions will combine to help you make your decision, but never just continue to provide a service out of reverence for tradition. Make sure that it makes good mission sense.

☞ **HANDS-ON:** Try this exercise. Take out your income and expense statement for last month. Look at the income side of the ledger for the year to date. Take the total income and multiply it by .8 (80 percent). Then, start with the largest customer, add that income to that of the second largest customer, then the third, and so on, until your running income total reaches the 80 percent threshold. Now, go back and count how many customers that took. If you now look at your entire customer base, you will find that the number of customers it took to reach the 80 percent is very close to one-fifth, or 20 percent.

E. FORMS ON THE COMPANION CD-ROM

Form 6-7 **Forms on the Companion CD-ROM**				
Form Name	**Form No.**	**Workbook Page**	**File Name**	**File Format**
Who Are Our Markets?	6-1	54	FORM0601.DOC	Word for Windows
Training Checklist—Marketing	6-2	55	FORM0602.DOC	Word for Windows
Marketing Checklist—Target Market Identification	6-3	56	FORM0603.DOC	Word for Windows
What Do Our Markets Really Want?	6-4	57	FORM0604.DOC	Word for Windows
Our Core Competencies	6-5	58	FORM0605.DOC	Word for Windows
Implementation Checklist	6-6	59	FORM0606.DOC	Word for Windows
Forms on the Companion CD-ROM	6-7	60	FORM0607.DOC	Word for Windows

● FORM0607.DOC

F. RESOURCES FOR FURTHER STUDY

Topic: Market Identification
Books
Strategic Marketing for NonProfit Organizations, 5th edition, by Philip Kotler, Alan Andreasen (contributor). Prentice Hall, 1995.
Software
Market Plan Pro: This program is really marketing planning software, but it asks all the right questions. You can also see a ton of marketing plans at *www.paloalto.com*.
Web Sites
The Free Management Library's information on market positioning: *www.mapnp.org/library/mrktng/position.htm*   Another free management site on business (including market) research: *www.mapnp.org/library/research/research.htm*
Online Courses
Nonprofit Self-Grassroots MBA This online set of classes is designed for you to take at your own speed, and it covers all kinds of management skills, including marketing: *www.mapnp.org/library/mgmnt/mba_prog.htm*

7

Your Competition

A. STRAIGHT FROM *MISSION-BASED MARKETING*

Here are a few important ideas from *Mission-Based Marketing* on the subject of your competition. Remember that mission-based organizations respect and embrace competition; they don't shy away from it.

Competition is a good thing. It is a hard thing, but it is good—for your organization and for the people you serve. Competition should make us provide better services to people in a more efficient, more effective, and more market-driven manner. Unfortunately, for many not-for-profits the idea of competition sends the entire organization into chaos. But remember, competition is not new to you. You have always competed for good staff, good board members, and donated dollars. You might now be forced to compete for people to serve, and if you embrace the idea of competing, you will be better for it. So will the people who you serve.

1. What You Need to Know about Your Competition

With your competitors, you need to find out important information that you can then use to become a better competitor yourself. You need to learn the following four core things about your competitors:

- *What services do they provide?* Do they compete with you across the board or only in certain areas? If they are a full-spectrum competitor, you probably need to investigate them more carefully than if they are only competing with you in one area (unless they are only providing your most profitable service).

- *What clientele are they seeking?* Do they target the same population that you do? Do they just take the most lucrative segment of your population, a technique known as creaming? On the other hand, do your target markets and theirs not really overlap? This factor is also important. If you are targeting people over 60, for example, and the competitor has that age cohort as a secondary or tertiary market, you might not have to worry as much.

- *What value do they give to the customer?* Remember, price is not the issue; value is. What does your competitor do that provides value to the customer? An added value at a museum might be a well-designed map or a number of easily accessible benches or restrooms. An added value for a counseling center might be a particularly friendly receptionist and free coffee in the receptionist's area. Whatever the competition is doing, is it something that you can also provide, provide well, and remain within your mission statement?

- *What are their prices?* Is the price truly comparable to yours, or do you (or they) offer more service for the same price? While price is not *the* issue (value always is), it is an important issue for many customers. Make doubly sure that you do your best to compare apples to apples when looking at price. Otherwise, you might make bad decisions based on the assumptions that your price is lower (or higher) than the competition's.

You need to find out about services, target markets, value, and prices at a minimum. It would also be nice to know about other things, but these are the core issues to look at first. How do you find out? You do a little market research aimed at your competition.

B. BASELINE SELF-ASSESSMENT

Form 7-1 **Competition Self-Assessment**	Yes	No
Have we identified our competitors for each of our target markets?	3	–1
Have we researched our competitors' strengths?	2	0
Have we identified our competitors' weaknesses?	2	0
Are we focusing on the same target markets as our competitors?	2	–1
Do we ask our network of board, staff, vendors, and funders about our competitors?	3	–1
Do we view competition as an inherently good thing?	4	–1
Do we have a system in place to alert us when new competition for our services arrives in our area?	3	0
Do we know our competitors' prices?	4	–1
Do we know what value they add to their services that we don't?	3	0
Do we know what value we add to our services that our competitors don't?	3	0
Total of Column Score (Add up each column and put the answer here.) ➜		
TOTAL SCORE (Add total scores from Yes and No columns and put the answer here.) ➜		

● FORM0701.DOC

SCORING ANALYSIS:
24–29 Excellent
19–23 Very Good
13–18 Adequate
Less than 13—You are not paying enough attention to your competition.

C. WORKSHEETS AND CHECKLISTS

Form 7-2   Assessment of Competition

The Services We Provide	Competitors	Where They Excel	Where We Excel
The People We Serve	**Competitors**	**Where They Excel**	**Where We Excel**

FORM0702.DOC

Form 7-3 Checklist—Competition

Y	Action	For Which Staff	Deadline	Responsible Person
	Identify all our payer competitors.			
	Identify all our service competitors.			
	Identify all our referral competitors.			
	Make a list of overlapping services, core competencies, and constituencies.			
	Develop business criteria.			
	Decide if we want to expand or diminish our head-on competition areas.			
	Decide areas in which we compete that we need to strengthen.			

● FORM0703.DOC

Form 7-4 Implementation Checklist Topic: Social Entrepreneurship		
Measurable Outcome	**Deadline**	**Person or Group Responsible**

● FORM0704.DOC

D. ☞ HANDS-ON

☞ **HANDS-ON:** While you are at it, check your own records. You can enter and edit information on Guidestar.com. You can edit and update information at the Secretary of State and IRS offices. Make sure that your information is up-to-date and accurate. When you run a search on a competitor, always run one on yourself—to find out what your competitor, and potential customers, are finding out about you.

☞ **HANDS-ON:** Think about the following issues related to your competition.

- *Board members.* Ask board members (and friends and neighbors) who are serving or have served on other boards what they like most and least about their board *service*. Don't ask detailed and pointed questions about the other organization— you might not get good information. Focus your questions on the functions of the board that they liked and disliked. If there are board workshops run through your United Way, community foundation, local management services organization (MSO), or local college or university nonprofit program, go to them and learn about the state of the art. You need to make your board service desirable.

- *Staff.* When staff members come aboard, ask them what they liked most and least about their previous jobs. When they leave, ask them in an exit interview what attracted them to their new job (or drove them away from your organization). Read the want ads to check salaries and benefits. Take part in salary surveys run by local or state trade associations or your state nonprofit association to get a handle on competitiveness.

- *Donations*. Be a constant observer of how you personally are asked for money, and urge your board and staff to do the same. Do you like being "hit up" in the super-market parking lot, by snailmail, by e-mail, by phone, or in person? Within these groupings, what approaches do you like and dislike? Do you give online? Does your staff or board do the same? Look at the printed material that other organizations are handing out, and see how they pitch for donations on their web site. What appeals to you, and what doesn't? The field of donations is incredibly competitive and sophisticated, and new innovations pop up all the time. Pay attention.

☞ **HANDS-ON:** When you talk to your volunteers, use a group session rather than individual meetings. Volunteers tend, for the most part, to be a bit awed by the senior management staff, and putting them in a peer group will not only make them more at ease but also generate more ideas and reactions for you. In addition, it saves you time.

E. FORMS ON THE COMPANION CD-ROM

Form 7-5 Forms on the Companion CD-ROM				
Form Name	**Form No.**	**Workbook Page**	**File Name**	**File Format**
Competition Self-Assessment	7-1	64	FORM0701.DOC	Word for Windows
Assessment of Competition	7-2	65	FORM0702.DOC	Word for Windows
Checklist for Competition	7-3	66	FORM0703.DOC	Word for Windows
Implementation Checklist	7-4	67	FORM0704.DOC	Word for Windows
Forms on the Companion CD-ROM	7-5	68	FORM0705.DOC	Word for Windows

● FORM0705.DOC

F. RESOURCES FOR FURTHER STUDY

Topic: Competition
Books
Here is the site on the John Wiley & Sons web site for books related to nonprofit competition. You'll get the latest list at this URL: *www.wiley.com/remsearch.cgi?query=nonprofit+competition&field=keyword*
Software
None as of this writing
Web Sites
The Free Management Library's take on competitive research: *www.mapnp.org/library/mrktng/cmpetitr/cmpetitr.htm* Marketing and Competitor Research: CEO Express is a great start for lots of sites. Scroll down to Business Research: *www.ceoexpress.com*
Online Courses
Nonprofit Self-Grassroots MBA This online set of classes is designed for you to take at your own speed, and it covers all kinds of management skills, including marketing: *www.mapnp.org/library/mgmnt/mba_prog.htm*

8

Asking Your Markets
What They Want

A. STRAIGHT FROM *MISSION-BASED MARKETING*

Here are a few important ideas from *Mission-Based Marketing* on the all-important subject of asking your markets. You need to ask to find out what people want. You need to ask regularly, consistently, and in the end, become a culture of asking.

1. No One Knows What a Market Wants Until Asking

The biggest single mistake that people make in marketing is saying, "I've been in this market for 20 years. I know what people want." The truth is that *no one knows all of what a market wants until asking, and they need to ask regularly.* Do you learn all new stuff when you ask? Of course not. Most of what you learn will confirm what you already know. But the new things, the changes in what markets want, will enable you to improve services to become more competitive. You have to ask, listen, and then respond.

2. Asking Is the Biggest Single Way to Avoid the Marketing Disability

In *Mission-Based Marketing,* I talk at length about the marketing disability—confusing wants and needs. In many not-for-profits, the focus is on needs assessment, not on what people want. Remember, people have needs, but people seek wants. The job of the mission-based marketer is to give people what they need in a way that they want it. And, as we saw in No. 1 above, you have to ask to find out what people want. You can start to overcome your marketing disability by asking, and then by listening, and then by responding.

B. BASELINE SELF-ASSESSMENT

Form 8-1 Asking Your Markets Self-Assessment	Yes	No
Do we ask our payers about their satisfaction with us at least annually?	3	0
Do we ask our service customers about their satisfaction with us at least annually?	3	0
Do we ask our staff about their job satisfaction at least every 18 months?	3	0
Do we ask our board about their satisfaction at least every 18 months?	3	0
Do we have a culture of asking?	2	–1
Do we train our staff in how to ask and how to listen?	2	0
Do we do focus groups to find/test new services and/or products?	2	0
Do we have a formal system to widely share information on complaints?	3	–1
Do we share the information we gather in surveys, focus groups, and interviews with staff and board?	3	–2
Do we track satisfaction quarter-to-quarter or year-to-year?	3	–1
Do we let the people we ask know the results of our inquiry, and what we've done with their ideas?	4	–2
Do we have a feedback loop on our web site?	2	–1
Total of Column Score (Add up each column and put the answer here.) ➜		
TOTAL SCORE (Add total scores from Yes and No columns and put the answer here.) ➜		

FORM0801.DOC

SCORING ANALYSIS:
26–33 Excellent
20–25 Very Good
12–19 Adequate
Less than 12—You are not focusing on asking adequately. Use the following tables and checklists to start moving your organization toward a culture of asking.

C. WORKSHEETS AND CHECKLISTS

Form 8-2 Marketing Checklist—Asking Informally

Y	Activity	Rationale	Deadline	Responsible Person
	Train all staff in how to ask regularly about customer satisfaction. Focus on sales, reception and marketing team first, then all staff.	You need to have a culture of asking.		
	Develop feedback loop to get information to the marketing team.	The information does no good if it doesn't get to the right people.		
	Empower staff to fix identified problems.	If you ask, people will point out ways to improve. Most issues can and should be resolved quickly.		

FORM0802.DOC

Form 8-3   Marketing Checklist—Asking with Surveys

Y	Activity	Rationale	Deadline	Responsible Person
	List the markets you want to survey, and how often.	Asking on a regular, standardized basis, is the only way to get defendable data that you can compare over time.		
	List what you want to know, but stay focused.	Remember you only have four minutes to survey, if you want people to respond!		
	Get some outside help to put the questions in the correct order and wording.	This is the time to get some expertise.		
	Put instructions on the front and end of the survey.	Tell people (briefly) why you are asking, when the deadline is, where to send the completed survey, and how to fill it out. And, say thank you!		
	Close the loop.	After you analyze the data, get back to the people you surveyed and tell them what you learned—it will increase your response rate next time.		
	Share the information internally.	You asked. You learned. Now, to improve, you have to let people know what you found out—the good news and the bad news.		

FORM0803.DOC

This is a survey that was used by an East Coast rehabilitation center to assess the satisfaction of their clients with services. It was administered by interview in the client's home, so they could get away with having it longer than usual.

Note that the numbers to the left of each question's answers are there to facilitate data entry. This was essentially a closed-choice survey. As you read it, you will see that in some cases there is a mixed choice for identifying the respondents. This is because in some cases the person with the disability was the respondent and, in some cases, it was the person's advocate.

Also note that this survey does not have (nor does it need) instructions at the beginning and the end of the survey. The reason for this is that the survey was administered by interview. If you send out surveys by mail, you *need* the instructions.

Form 8-4 **Survey Sample**

Date_____

Client name_____

Parent/guardian name_____

Client's age_____

1. **Who is responding to this questionnaire? (Please circle the number.)**
   4 Consumer
   3 Family member
   2 Guardian
   1 Advocate
   0 Other: _____

2. **Sex of respondent**
   2 Female
   1 Male

3. **Indicate this person's primary disability.**
   5 Mental retardation
   4 Cerebral palsy
   3 Epilepsy
   2 Autism
   1 Other: _____
   0 Don't know

4. **Where does this person live?**
   6 Residential facility   Please describe: _____
   5 Parent's home
   4 Guardian's home
   3 Conservator's home
   2 On his/her own (with residential support)
   1 On his/her own (no support)
   0 Other _____

5. Do you know what The Center is?
   2 Yes
   1 No
   0 Not sure

6. When did you/_____ (insert name of client) first come in contact with The Center?
   5 Less than 6 months
   4 6 months to 2 years
   3 2 to 5 years
   2 5 to 10 years
   1 More than 10 years
   0 Don't know

7. Do you know your client program coordinator's name?
   2 Yes
   1 No
   0 Don't know

8. How well did your coordinator explain your/_____'s rights and the services available to you?
   4 Explained very well
   3 Explained somewhat
   2 Not well explained
   1 Not explained at all
   0 Don't know

9. How satisfied are you with the assessment and the services that were recommended for you/_____ ?
   5 Very satisfied
   4 Somewhat satisfied
   3 Neutral/It's OK
   2 Somewhat dissatisfied
   1 Very dissatisfied
   0 Not sure

10. Do you feel your coordinator is acting on your/_____'s behalf in obtaining services for you?
   4 Yes, very much
   3 Yes, somewhat
   2 No, not very much
   1 No, not at all
   0 Not sure

(continued)

11. **What services are you/is _____ receiving as a result of The Center's assessment and referrals?**

   _____

   _____

   _____

   _____

12. **What providers are currently bringing these services to you/_____?**

   _____

   _____

   _____

   _____

13. **Does The Center contact you regularly to discuss your/_____'s progress?**
   - 3   Yes
   - 2   No
   - 1   Sometimes
   - 0   Don't know

14. **Have you contacted The Center about any questions or problems you have had?**
   - 2   Yes
   - 1   No
   - 0   Don't know/Don't remember

15. **If yes, how helpful was the coordinator in solving your problems?**
   - 5   Very helpful
   - 4   Somewhat helpful
   - 3   Not very helpful
   - 2   Not helpful at all
   - 1   I have not contacted The Center concerning a problem
   - 0   Don't know/Don't remember

16. **When you call The Center with a problem or question, how soon does the client program coordinator respond?**
   - 5   Within 24 hours
   - 4   Within 1 week
   - 3   Within 2 weeks
   - 2   More than 2 weeks
   - 1   I have not contacted The Center concerning a problem
   - 0   Don't know

17. Did you feel this action was fast enough to address your situation?
- 3 No
- 2 Yes
- 1 I have not contacted The Center concerning a problem
- 0 Don't know

18. Are you satisfied with the amount of time your case manager spends with you/_____?
- 5 Very satisfied
- 4 Somewhat satisfied
- 3 Neutral/It's OK
- 2 Somewhat dissatisfied
- 1 Very dissatisfied
- 0 Not sure

19. Have you/has _____ received the assistance you hoped for since you/he/she began working with The Center?
- 4 Yes, definitely
- 3 Probably
- 2 Probably not
- 1 Definitely not
- 0 Not sure

20. Would you refer another person with a disability to The Center?
- 2 Yes
- 1 No
- 0 Don't know

21. What three things do you think The Center does best?

_____

_____

_____

22. What three things do you think The Center could do better?

_____

_____

_____

Form 8-5 Marketing Checklist—Asking Focus Groups

Y	Activity	Rationale	Deadline	Responsible Person
	Choose the target markets you will want to focus on.	Pick carefully, as focus groups are great, but expensive.		
	Pick homogeneous groups to participate.	Don't mix people—staff and funders, or business people and clients, for example.		
	Get a facilitator.	You need an outsider for these sessions.		
	Hold the session in a safe, neutral location.	Sounds obvious, but people regularly forget this.		
	Have the facilitator ask your questions in a priority order.	Ask your most important question third.		
	Audio tape the session, but don't videotape it.	You need the record, but the camera really inhibits many people.		

FORM0805.DOC

Form 8-6 Implementation Checklist Topic: Asking Your Markets		
Measurable Outcome	Deadline	Person or Group Responsible

● FORM0806.DOC

D. ☞ HANDS-ON

☞ **HANDS-ON:** When you do change parts of your surveys, make sure that you note it in the report. For example, let's assume that your previous consumer surveys only had four choices in a question that asked, "Which of our programs do you use the most?" and that your current survey gives six choices, because you have added two new services since your last survey. This change, while valid and worthwhile, will skew the comparative data; thus, the change deserves a notation in the report. Always make such notations to be fair to the reader. And, if the only reader is going to be you, *still* make the notations so that in future years you can remember what changed.

☞ **HANDS-ON:** Warning, warning, warning! Your executive director or board president will ask you to make your survey longer, saying something like, "Since we're sending out the survey anyway, let's save some money and throw in a few questions on one or two other subjects." Resist! Blame me! Not only does this action soak up the limited time people will give you to fill out the survey, but it also causes you to lose the focus you have worked so hard to acquire in the survey. Fewer people return the survey, and it is less focused. Thus, you don't save money and waste it instead.

☞ **HANDS-ON:** When making a list of what you need to know for a survey, particularly in the area of identifiers, make a list of the breakouts you would like to see. These categories might be organized by gender, age group, ethnicity, location of service, or countless other "slices" of information. Then, look at the list and for each item on it ask the questions, "What am I going to do with this information? Am I collecting it from curiosity or need? Will I be able to use the information that I collect?" Be brutal on yourself in this area. The strong tendency for people is to ask for too much information. I have read countless survey reports that are demographically loaded but light on real information. The reports nearly describe the shoe size of the respondents but don't have much hard information that is of use. Make a list, and ask "Why?" before including the identifier in the final survey.

☞ **HANDS-ON:** When you do change parts of your surveys, make sure that you note it in the report. For example, let's assume that your previous consumer surveys only had 4 choices in a question that asked, "Which of our programs do you use the most?", and your current survey gives 6 choices, as you have added two new services since your last survey. This change, while valid and worthwhile, will skew the comparative data, and thus the change deserves a notation in the report. Always make such notations to be fair to the reader. And, if the only reader is going to be you, still make the notations, so that in future years, you can remember what changed!

☞ **HANDS-ON:** You have just imposed on the people who gave you valuable information. Do the right thing. Tell them what you learned. Send a memo to folks, or put a report in your newsletter. Or, just make an announcement at a staff meeting, but let people know that you asked and that you appreciated their input. Be sure to list the key things that the most people said. Make a list of what you learned, and then tell people what you are doing about it. It might look something like Exhibit 8-1 below:

Exhibit 8-1 Asking for Feedback

We learned the following things and have taken the following actions:	
Items A, B, C, D	We have already implemented changes to respond to these excellent ideas.
Items E, F, H, J	We are budgeting these for the next fiscal year.
Items G, I, L	We cannot accommodate these suggestions because of regulatory restraints.
Items K, M	The Board will discuss these policy change ideas at their next meeting.

You not only allow people to learn from each other, but you also acknowledge their input and take credit for taking action—something about which most people are pretty cynical. They often assume that their ideas go into a large trash barrel. So don't do that. Instead, tell them what you heard, and equally importantly what you have done about it. Show them that you are responsive.

E. FORMS ON THE COMPANION CD-ROM

Form 8-7 Forms on the Companion CD-ROM

Form Name	Form No.	Workbook Page	File Name	File Format
Asking Self-Assessment	8-1	71	FORM0801.DOC	Word for Windows
Marketing Checklist—Asking Informally	8-2	72	FORM0802.DOC	Word for Windows
Marketing Checklist—Asking with Surveys	8-3	73	FORM0803.DOC	Word for Windows
Sample Survey	8-4	74–77	FORM0804.DOC	Word for Windows
Checklist—Asking Focus Groups	8-5	78	FORM0805.DOC	Word for Windows
Implementation Checklist	8-6	79	FORM0806.DOC	Word for Windows
Forms on the Companion CD-ROM	8-7	81	FORM0807.DOC	Word for Windows

● FORM0807.DOC

F. RESOURCES FOR FURTHER STUDY

Topic: Asking

Books
Focus Groups: A Practical Guide for Applied Research, 3rd edition, by Richard A. Krueger and Mary Anne Casey. Sage Publications, April 2000. (ISBN 0761920714). *Developing Questions for Focus Groups* (Focus Group Kit, Vol. 3) by Richard A. Krueger. Sage Publications, September 1997. (ISBN 0761908196). *Moderating Focus Groups: A Practical Guide for Group Facilitation* by Thomas L. Greenbaum. Sage Publications, November 1999. (ISBN 0761920447). *Mail and Internet Surveys: The Tailored Design Method, 2nd edition*, by Don A. Dillman. John Wiley & Sons, November 1999. (ISBN 0471323543). *How to Conduct Surveys: A Step-by-Step Guide, 2nd edition*, by Arlene Fink and Jacqueline B. Kosecoff. Sage Publications, April 1998. (ISBN 0761914099). *Internet Research Surveys Via Web and Email* by Matthias Schonlau, Ronald D. Fricker, and Marc N. Elliott. Rand Corporation, June 2001. (ISBN 0833031104).

Software
Development software: Here's a couple of links to listings of fund-raising software with reviews: *www.techsoup.org/articles.cfm?topicid=2&topic=Software* *http://nonprofit.about.com/cs/npofrsoftware/index.htm?terms=fundraising+software*

Web Sites
These three sites help you do online surveys (small ones for free and large ones for a fee): *www.statpac.com/online-surveys* *http://free-online-surveys.co.uk* *www.zoomerang.com* Fundraising resources on the Web: A very thorough site that includes information on software, consultants, organizations, and other resources is: *www.agrm.org/dev-trak/links.html*.

Online Courses
Nonprofit Self-Grassroots MBA This online set of classes is designed for you to take at your own speed, and it covers all kinds of management skills, including marketing: *www.mapnp.org/library/mgmnt/mba_prog.htm*

9

Better Marketing Materials

You've done a whole lot of work already: figuring out who your markets are, asking them what they want, and looking at ways to improve the value of your services compared to your competition. But now that you've done all that, you still have to pay attention to the entire area of letting people know that you exist, that your services are available, and that you can solve their problems. That is what marketing materials are.

A. STRAIGHT FROM *MISSION-BASED MARKETING*

Marketing "material" covers a lot of ground. It can be the traditional three-fold brochure or stacked handouts that come in a large folder. It can be advertising in a local newspaper or magazine or a flyer that is placed under a windshield wiper. It can be your business card or your web site. It can be your promotional spot on local television or radio, the notices you send out in direct mail, or the educational materials that you give free of charge to the people you serve in person or online. It can be information on memberships, donations, or even a promotional trinket such as a key chain, calendar, or coffee mug. For most readers, their organization will be promoted through a mix of these vehicles in addition to word of mouth, referrals, and straight sales.

But whatever it is, the mix has to address some similar issues. Many not-for-profits, like their for-profit peers, do a great job at developing and appropriately using their marketing materials. Many, however, do not. Also, many not-for-profits are still doing that job as if they are living in the old, less-competitive economy. They focus on *public relations* and *promotion* rather than *marketing*. There is an enormous difference.

Also, there is an overarching rule for marketing material: it must connect with the targeted market from the customer's point of view. In other words, good marketing material grabs the customer and shows that person that you understand his or her wants, who he or she is, and that you can solve his or her problems. By reading your brochure, listening to your radio spot, or looking at your web site, can the customer quickly understand the benefit of using your organization's services? If not, you have not made the connection.

The Problems with Most Not-for-Profit Marketing Material

You have already read that the critical sequence in marketing is identifying your markets, asking those markets what they want, and then developing or amending services to meet those wants. This is called being *market-oriented,* and it is much preferable to being *service-oriented* (where an organization just pushes its available services with little regard to what the market wants).

Here is the problem. Most of the marketing material that I see is *service-oriented,* pushing the existing service array, usually in jargon, and hardly ever in a way that really appeals to the wants of the markets. It is dull, dense, and not of interest to too many people beyond the individual who wrote it. It is also often poorly written, unprofessional looking, and out of date. It doesn't spell out the benefits of using the organization and makes no attempt to connect with the customer.

Why, in an era of dirt-cheap, easy-to-use software and excellent low-cost color printers, do not-for-profits scrimp on marketing material? Why shoot yourself in the foot every time a potential customer, donor, referral source, banker, or board member sees an advertisement or promotional piece? Because we continue to confuse needs with wants and continue to try to do things cheaply—when actually we're wasting money.

Things to Include in Your Marketing Material

Now, let's turn to a list of things that you should make sure are included in your marketing material. I would suggest that your marketing committee review all of your materials, commercials, handouts, and presentations for the following seven components. Also, remember that you have to *connect with your customer,* showing him or her the benefits of using your services.

1. *Your mission.* If your mission statement (or charitable purpose) is succinct and not full of jargon, it is an excellent thing to include in most of your marketing material. If it is so long that it will take up 90 percent of your space, forget it. But your mission is the defining statement of what and who your organization is, and you should be able to lead with it.
2. *Focus.* Each piece of marketing material should be focused on a target market or a service component. The art museum in the previous example could develop a piece for art lovers, parents, and art teachers. That would be an example of focusing on a target market. A YMCA might have a piece on summer camp, one on its aerobics classes, and one on its basketball and soccer leagues. That would be an example of focus on a service. But, and this point is very important, even within the "service pieces" it is critical that you use terms that connect to the market wants. If you just focus on the service, you are back to that service-oriented rather than market-oriented mentality. We will talk more about different materials for different markets in a few pages.
3. *Brevity.* Blessed is the person who can say it in the fewest, clearest words. Remember that no one is forcing the reader to spend the time reading your material. It needs to be *brief,* or they will get bored and stop reading. You should have no run-on sentences or minute details. Give the essential information only. With all appropriate apologies to the English majors among you, your role model for your printed material (not your web site, which can be much more detailed) should be *USA Today,* which is heavy on bullets and does not have too many sentences with commas. Keep it short, and keep people's attention.

4. *Connection*. Does the material clearly show that your organization understands the problems of the target market(s)? Does it clearly state that you can help solve those problems? If not, you are trusting the reader to make those connections, and that is a mistake.

5. *Appearance*. As I mentioned earlier, there is no excuse for sloppy material, poor writing, and cheap-looking paper or graphics. They speak volumes about your organization. Word processing and printing are so inexpensive now that there is little impediment in your way to developing professional-looking materials at a reasonable cost.

6. *References*. In certain materials, it will be important to list well-known customers. For example, if you are a health care organization, it might be important to list the large employers with whose employee health plans you qualify or the managed care plans. Other organizations need to make connections to state and national associations to show a level of quality ("Certified by the National Association of XYZ") or to a community standard ("A United Way Agency"). As with your other text, be brief and put only those references that mean something to the target market for that particular marketing piece. For example, being accredited by the Joint Commission on the Accreditation of Hospitals might be important to a referring physician but meaningless to a patient. Be selective and focused.

7. *A source for more information*. Always include a location where people can call for more information. Include a phone number, hours of availability, *and the name* (not the title) of the person to contact. I realize that this means that you will have to update the materials when that person changes jobs, but the personal listing is valuable in two ways. First, it is just that—personal—and gives a name to an otherwise impersonal organization. Second, it routes the questions to the right person immediately. One thing that nearly all of us despise is being put on hold or being handed off endlessly from person to person trying to find out some simple fact, figure, time, or other answer to our question. By putting the name of the correct person on the brochure, you simplify the process and usually avoid the problem.

All of these things should show up in some fashion in your material. Now, let's look at the other side of the coin.

Things to Avoid in Your Marketing Material

I assume that you have now gone through your material to make sure that these items are included. But there might well be things that are in your material that you should pull out. There are certainly things to avoid. I provide you with a list of seven common items that you should keep out of your material:

1. *Jargon*. The worst offense in marketing material is to speak in a language that people don't understand. You don't impress people by confusing them. Using jargon puts a big barrier between you and most audiences. I have long contended that if you can't explain or describe what you do in words that a fourth grader can understand, you don't really understand what you do. Simplify, clarify, and remember that the average American reads on a mid-high school level.

   Having said that, there is a time for jargon. If your marketing material is targeted toward professionals in the field, jargon is the language of the profession and is thus appropriate. If, for example, you were developing a brochure to advertise a continuing education program in computers, the terms DOS, ASCII, PC, icons, Internet, and modem would probably be appropriate. If you were training on labor law, citing the laws and using common labor law terms and issues would be important. Write for your audience.

2. *Inappropriate photos*. Here is the sad truth. Most people don't care about how your building looks. You do, because you probably have put a great deal of blood, sweat, tears, energy, and money into the property. But most pictures of buildings are a waste of precious space in a marketing brochure. Pictures of people are usually much more effective, but even those can be counterproductive if they are grainy, unfocused, or so small as to be unrecognizable. Make sure that each and every photo (or graphic) that you include is valuable, and like the text, simple, focused, and understandable. Also make sure that for any image of any person you use in any media (print or online) that you have a valid, current, signed photo release.

3. *Lack of focus*. There is nothing wrong with a general-purpose brochure, but there is something definitely wrong with having *just* a general-purpose brochure or having a general-purpose brochure that tries to do everything for everyone. Focus is the heart of good marketing material. Ask yourself, "What is the purpose of this piece of paper?" If the piece goes much beyond that central purpose, it is almost certainly unfocused and too long.

4. *Asking for money*. With the exception of fundraising letters and brochures, whose focus is explaining the various ways to give to your organization, asking for money is outside the core purpose of the marketing material and thus out of focus. I know that it is tempting to just throw in a sentence or two about donations, particularly if you are desperate for money, but that desperation will come through—and some markets might well be turned off. Stick with your focus.

5. *A history lesson*. Few people care about your organization's history or even how long you have been in existence. Having said that, some organizations need to validate their experience and stability by saying things like, "Serving the Finger Lakes Region since 1965." But more often, I see people who use 400 words to explain the origins of their organization in great (and agonizing) detail. They list the initial incorporators, the first few office addresses, and even give pictures of some of the sites that they have occupied, noting additional important dates in history. There is nothing wrong with history, and we certainly can learn from it. But is a recitation of your organization's past (however laudable) "on-message" for the marketing piece you are developing? Probably not, but if it is, is your recounting of the development of your organization brief and readable? Stay focused.

6. *Out of date*. I really love pictures of staff, board, and service recipients in bell bottoms, with shag haircuts or in leisure suits. They make me want to run right down to the disco. The problem is that the disco is closed—a part of the past. Pictures that are from a bygone era will set you up for ridicule, not respect. They will disenchant people, and they will wonder whether it is your programs or just your photos that are outdated. Again, in this era of quick and easy software that includes photos at the click of a mouse, there is no excuse for having your brochure look like a retrospective.

7. *Boring.* If you wrote the text in a particular piece, you probably won't be a good judge of how interesting your information is. Get it read by people inside and outside the organization. Ask hard questions: "Is this boring? Does it run on? Can we say more in less words? Are we 'on-message,' focused, and keeping connected with the intended audience?" Don't trust your own instincts here. Get a few outside opinions. I usually am pretty happy with my own writing, but it is *always* improved by the friends, coworkers, and (in the case of my books) editors who read it. Get an outside opinion or three. It will help you avoid the dreaded B word.

B. BASELINE SELF-ASSESSMENT

Form 9-1 Marketing Materials Self-Assessment		
	Yes	No
Do we focus on one general purpose brochure?	–4	2
Do we have targeted materials for our three top payer markets?	3	–1
Do we have targeted materials for our three top service markets?	3	–2
Do we have printed materials that focus on our referral sources?	3	–3
Is all of our marketing material reviewed and updated at least anually?	3	–2
Does all of our marketing material include contact name, phone number, web site, and e-mail information?	4	–3
Do we have a web site?	5	–5
Is our web site checked every 30 days for currency?	2	–2
Do we have special sections on our web site for board, staff, and education of service recipients?	3	–2
Do we invest in staff training in how to design and print our own marketing materials?	4	0
Do we have printed material that focuses only on fund raising?	2	0
Do we have printed materials to help recruit volunteers?	2	0
Have we reviewed our agency "look" (color, logo, font, paper type) in the past three years?	3	–1
Total of Column Score (Add up each column and put the answer here.) ➔		
TOTAL SCORE (Add total scores from Yes and No columns and put the answer here.) ➔		

FORM0901.DOC

SCORING ANALYSIS:

30–39 Excellent
23–30 Very Good
16–22 Adequate
Less than 16—You need to focus on your marketing materials—and soon.

C. WORKSHEETS AND CHECKLISTS

Form 9-2 **Marketing Materials Training**				
Y	**Training Type**	**For Which Staff**	**Deadline**	**Responsible Person**
	Marketing Materials	Marketing Team		
	Improving Web Site Design	Marketing Team		
	Desktop Publishing	Marketing Team (Often offered by the software manufacturers or printer manufacturers. Check their web sites.)		
	Newsletter Development	Marketing Team		

FORM0902.DOC

Form 9-3 **Marketing Checklist—Marketing Materials**

Check and see that your marketing materials have the characteristics that are checked, and don't have the characteristics with the X's. If there are things that need to be fixed, put them on the form.

Y	Good Characteristic	What Needs to Be Fixed	Deadline	Responsible Person
Y	Your mission statement			
Y	Focus on one issue or market			
Y	Brevity			
Y	Connecting problems and solutions			
Y	Professional appearance			
Y	A source for more information (name, phone number, and e-mail)			

Y	Bad Characteristic	What Needs to Be Fixed	Deadline	Responsible Person
Y	Jargon (Can high school students understand every word?)			
Y	Inappropriate photos (old ones that you don't have releases for)			
Y	Lack of focus (blah, blah, blah)			
Y	Asking for money (except in a fund-raising piece)			
Y	Out of date (Do you mention Y2K, the bicentennial, or going into the new millenium?)			
Y	Boring (Again ask your high schoolers.)			

● FORM0903.DOC

Form 9-4   Marketing Checklist—Web Site

Y	Activity	Rationale	Deadline	Responsible Person
	Do you have a web site?	Welcome to the twenty-first century.		
	Does it include information that is in more depth than your printed materials?	There is no point in just reprinting your printed materials electronically. A web site is an incredible resource that takes work. You can't just set it and forget it.		
	Does it allow for people to contact you electronically? Does someone check the e-mail?	You want every available way for people to get in touch and find out more.		
	Can people make donations online?	A must.		
	Is the web site checked for accuracy and currency every two weeks?	Things go out of date fast.		
	Do you regularly (monthly) check other peer web sites for good ideas?	Don't reinvent the wheel, and be aware of what your competition is doing.		

FORM0904.DOC

Form 9-5 Implementation Checklist Topic: Marketing Materials		
Measurable Outcome	**Deadline**	**Person or Group Responsible**

● FORM0905.DOC

D. ☞ HANDS-ON

☞ **HANDS-ON:** Try this jargon test. Hand your marketing material to a neighbor or friend who knows *nothing* about your services. Ask them to read it carefully, circling every word that they do not *fully* understand. Make sure that they know that this exercise is not a test of their knowledge but a way of helping you make your materials more understandable. Try this activity with two or three friends and include your newsletters if you print those. Don't overload individuals, just give them one or two things each to review. You will learn a lot about what is jargon and what isn't.

☞ **HANDS-ON:** When was your marketing material last revised? Your web site? Your logo, slogan, letterhead, and other items? If you can't remember, or can't find the documents, it's too long ago. Refresh your materials now. It's cheap, and we'll spend part of the next chapter giving you lots of specifics on how to take advantage of the benefits of low-cost technology in this area.

☞ **HANDS-ON:** Never ever assume that a market will make the connection between your resources and their problem. They won't. And, in fairness, it's not their job—it's yours. In asking the market about what their wants are, you should be asking about their problems. This information comes best through the focus groups and informal asking that we discussed in Chapter 8, but also it comes through reading the general and business press. You will read, for example, about the problems of Americans feeling that their days are too short. What is the lesson? If you can save them time, you can attract them. You will read about their concerns about education and the breakup of the family. Can your organization make a connection here? Do you provide some kind of educational experience? Do you focus on the family unit in a definable way? If you do, these "buzz words" should show up in your marketing material.

☞ **HANDS-ON:** I have the best way to get a real-world, inexpensive read on two issues: boring and jargon. Get a group of 5-7 high school sophomores (not juniors, not seniors, not freshmen) and sit them down with a pizza, some soda, and your printed marketing materials. Ask them to read through your materials and to circle any words that they don't understand, and have them tell you in no uncertain terms what they feel is boring about your materials. Trust me, they will. Sophomores are 15 or 16 years old, and they are not worldly enough to have heard most of your jargon, but they are old enough to *love* telling adults when they are wrong. Try this exercise. Lots of my clients have, and it really works.

E. FORMS ON THE COMPANION CD-ROM

Form 9-6   Forms on the Companion CD-ROM

Form Name	Form No.	Workbook Page	File Name	File Format
Marketing Materials Self-Assessment	9-1	88	FORM0901.DOC	Word for Windows
Training Checklist— Marketing	9-2	89	FORM0902.DOC	Word for Windows
Marketing Materials Checklist	9-3	90	FORM0903.DOC	Word for Windows
Web Site Checklist	9-4	91	FORM0904.DOC	Word for Windows
Implementation Checklist	9-5	92	FORM0905.DOC	Word for Windows
Forms on the Companion CD-ROM	9-6	93	FORM0906.DOC	Word for Windows

FORM0906.DOC

F. RESOURCES FOR FURTHER STUDY

Topic: Marketing Materials

Books
Creating Brochures & Booklets (Graphic Design Basics) by Val Adkins, 128 pages, 1st edition. North Light Books, March 1994. (ISBN 0891345175).

Software
Check out this site—it reviews desktop publishing software: *www.desktoppublishing.com/reviews*   Hint: Also check with your software firm for online or local in-person training.

Web Sites
Printers: This site, run by Xerox, gives high-end printers to organizations who qualify—not by being a not-for-profit but by having enough volume of copies—and there is always a catch. You have to buy the toner cartridges. *www.freecolorprinters.com*   **Desktop Publishing:** A really good resource on how to do desktop brochure development: *http://desktoppub.about.com/cs/brochures*   The free management library's organizational communications links: *www.mapnp.org/library/commskls/cmm_writ.htm*

Online Courses
Nonprofit Self Grassroots MBA This online set of classes is designed for you to take at your own speed, and it covers all kinds of management skills, including marketing: *www.mapnp.org/library/mgmnt/mba_prog.htm*   Check out training opportunities for desktop publishing training: *http://desktoppublishing.com/training.html*

10

Technology and Marketing

It's a tech, tech, tech world, and using technology as part of your marketing effort is crucial. Tech has made it easier and cheaper for you to market, but also provides some pot holes into which you can fall. Here are some of the key issues from *Mission-Based Marketing*.

A. STRAIGHT FROM *MISSION-BASED MARKETING*

Using Technology to Market in a Better, Faster, and More Focused Manner

So what are the things you can use technology for in your marketing efforts? There are tons, and the number and resulting benefits are growing every day. You can take donations online, e-mail your best customers, make your organization financially and programmatically transparent on your web site, and update your marketing material weekly and print it yourself at a lower cost with more focus. You can keep in touch with your volunteers, staff, and board markets through targeted web sites, and you can stay on everyone in the community's mind with an electronic newsletter. You can do all that and much, much more. But I am sure that some of you are thinking, "Yeah, yeah, yeah. But the people *we* serve don't have computers, don't have e-mail. What's the big deal?" Well, besides the fact that your staff and board almost certainly have some access to the Internet and to e-mail, technology still can help you do your promotional materials better. You might be surprised about the people you serve.

☐ **FOR EXAMPLE:** The events in this story occurred in late 1999, which was the Dark Ages in terms of Internet access. A friend of mine who runs a huge homeless shelter on the East Coast and who, like me, is a bit of a tech-head, called me late one night to tell me about a person who had checked in earlier that evening. My friend does intake once a month to keep himself close to the people his organization serves, and a person who (according to my friend) "was a caricature of a homeless man, the person a group of 4th graders would draw if asked to draw a homeless man" showed up at the intake desk. My friend checked him in, and because it was the first time this man had used this particular shelter, he asked him how he heard about the shelter and why he had chosen to come. The man looked at him for a second and said, "Well, I was, y'know, surfing the Web, and I came across your web site, and it looked good, so I, like, came over."

Where does a homeless person surf the Web? You know, don't you...at the library. I've told that story 100 times in training sessions, and when I tell it *everyone* laughs—I assume with surprise—and yet *everyone* knows the answer to the question of where the homeless man got online. Nevertheless, we continue to believe that the Internet doesn't affect us. It does. And don't forget, this story occurred way back in 1999.

Remember, too, that access to your organization online doesn't limit itself to just the people you serve. Go back to your list of markets. What about your funders? Your donors? Your volunteers? Your staff? Most if not all of them have the ability, even the desire, to access you in a variety of right-now ways. The people you serve are a *vital* market, but they are not your *only* market.

So, technology can help us market better. But, as I said earlier, it should not be an excuse to not do the basics of marketing such as asking, listening, and responding. Worse, tech can and does get in the way of good service.

Let's look at some specific areas where you can do more sooner, better, faster, and cheaper.

1. Data gathering/research

We have an encyclopedia at home for our children—actually two sets, one upstairs and one downstairs where our family computer is. 99 percent of the time, our kids ignore these resources, because the net is faster, deeper, and most importantly a habit for them. I have to regularly remind them that there is good information in print resources. "Yeah, how quaint, Dad."

Despite my old-fashioned love of printed things (like this book), for much of the information you want the net *is* the place to go. Want to find out what the state of the art is in a certain kind of brochure or web site? Go online. Need to know about best practices or benchmarking in your area of service? You can find that on the Web. Want to investigate which government or foundation funding is available for a program you want to provide? There are at least four web sites that do that for federal and state funding and will even e-mail you alerts when your keywords are "hit" by their software. Want to find out about your competitors? There are resources through your state economic development agency and your chamber of commerce as well as commercial sites galore.

Using the net for research is one of the prime benefits of being online. Use the resources that are there and that are improving every day.

2. Online access

I assume that your organization has a web site, but how much time have you spent looking at it from the point of view of being your first point of access? You want to allow people to access some of the things you do online. Why? We live in a right-now society. More and more people are used to checking you out online. You need to not only have basic information on your services, like locations and the like, but also think about ways you can add value with your web site. Here are some questions to consider:

• Can people find out about our locations, hours, and services easily on our web site (within two clicks of opening your main page)? Can they get directions and print a map?

- Can people sign up for appointments, purchase tickets, or check their grades (whatever is appropriate to your organization) online?

- Are there sources of information on your site for people to learn more about the issues that concern your organization? For instance, if your core service is foster care, is there a deep set of resources on becoming a foster parent, adoption, and so on?

- Is there information on staff, at least enough to let potential customers feel more at ease with the person who might help them? Do you include pictures and a short biography?

- Can volunteers (current or potential) explore options of things that they can do to help your organization?

- Can donors donate online? Can such donations be restricted by the donor?

- Can a funder see your current letters of accreditation, licenses, and any other quality assurances online (for example, as a scanned document)?

I'm sure as you read this you can think of many other things that could reach out to people who access you online, meet their wants, and impress them with your ability to solve their problems. And, of course, don't be afraid to ask people what they want from your web site. They'll give you great feedback and useful improvements to consider.

3. Staff, board, and customer e-mail

One of the few television shows I regularly watch is "Law & Order," which over the past few years has been on, it seems, 24 hours a day in reruns. As I was writing this chapter, I saw an episode from 1998 where one of the younger detectives was using something new—"some electronic mail thingy" in the words of an older detective—in an effort to solve a crime. It reminded me how far we have come in a short time. While not all of our board, staff, and customers have e-mail, most do—and for them, communication by e-mail is *expected and preferred*.

What can you do in terms of marketing and e-mail? Basically, two things: communicate quickly, inexpensively, and efficiently and keep your organizational presence in front of people without printing and postage expenses. Here are a number of things to consider, most of which have been tried and found useful by a number of my client organizations.

Weekly e-mail updates on regular issues. This could go to board staff and volunteers and could include a brief update on meetings for the week (perhaps split into staff, board, and volunteer areas, information on where minutes from last week's (or month's) meetings can be found on the organization's web site, announcements of new staff, retirements, certifications, awards, etc. This e-mail should be short but could eventually transition into an online newsletter; see section F).

Reminders of meetings. These reminders can increase attendance and preparation. A short e-mail reminding people of the place, time, subject, and agenda for a meeting, as well as what they should be bringing with them and/or have prepared is essential.

Requests for input/assistance. If you need resources from the community, ask your volunteers and staff for help. An e-mail is quick and can be just the trick to get their attention and have them respond to you quickly.

Job postings. Again, letting all staff, board, and volunteers know you are looking to fill a position can help spread the network wider. You already have trouble finding and keeping good staff, so why not use this method to jump start the process?

Customer updates. I would guarantee that all of your paying customers (funders, foundations, and state and local governments) both have and regularly use their e-mail. So, why not use the medium to communicate the good things about your organization, such as certifications, awards, and new services?

4. Telecommunications

Now, let's talk about phones, pagers, and automated telephone answering systems. Phones, pagers, and voice mail help us have access to staff (on the management side) and give access to customers (on the marketing side). In order to provide customer satisfaction, you need to make sure you can fix any problems that arise quickly. In our current right-now environment, you have to find out about the problem, get to the staff who can fix the problem, and let the customer know it has been fixed—soon. Telecommunications is a very important part of marketing and keeping close to your customers. Use it, but use it wisely. That's quite a list but only part of how technology can help you in doing better marketing.

B. BASELINE SELF-ASSESSMENT

Form 10-1 Self-Assessment—Technology & Marketing	Yes	No
Do we maintain e-mail lists of our donors, contacts, supporters, funders, etc?	3	–1
Do we design, edit, amend, update, and print our own marketing materials?	3	0
Do we give staff who need phones/pagers the tools to stay in touch?	3	–3
Do we regularly compare our web site's content, look, and ease of use with our peer organizations?	2	–1
Do we have an online newsletter?	2	0
Does our web site have the ability to accept donations?	4	–3
Do potential volunteers have a way to contact us through our web site?	1	–1
Do we have the ability to survey (and collate the data) online?	1	–1
Do we have a live person answering the phone during business hours? Do callers reach this person first, before getting a recording?	3	–5
Do we have voice mail for staff?	3	–1
Do we have good virus protection for all of our computers? (No point in sending viruses to your best customers!)	4	–4
Do we regularly check for updates and patches on our e-mail, word processing, publishing, accounting, and fund-raising software?	3	–1
Have we asked our payers, vendors, and staff if they would like to be paid through direct deposit and/or billed online?	3	0
Total of Column Score (Add up each column and put the answer here.) ➔		
TOTAL SCORE (Add total scores from Yes and No columns and put the answer here.) ➔		

● FORM1001.DOC

SCORING ANALYSIS:
28–35 Excellent
20–27 Very Good
14–19 Adequate
Less than 14—You need to pay more attention to the use of
technology in your marketing efforts.

As you start working your way through technology issues and marketing, here are some questions you can ask yourself and your marketing team:

- Do we use technology well in our pursuit of marketing?

- Are there ways we can keep in touch with our markets better through e-mail?

- Should we develop/expand an electronic newsletter?

- What can we do better on our web site? Should we have staff, board, and volunteer-specific areas of the site?

- Can and should we offer the opportunity for donations online? Why or why not?

- Do we have the software, hardware, and knowledge to try doing our own marketing materials? Can we go to some workshops on this issue and give it a try? How much do we spend a year on printing now? Could we cut that significantly?

- Are there better ways to survey and track the data we gather? Can we use off-the-shelf software, spreadsheets, or other tools to use the data better?

- What regular research do we do on our competition? Can we do more online?

C. WORKSHEETS AND CHECKLISTS

	Form 10-2 **Training Checklist—Technology & Marketing**			
Y	**Training Type**	**For Which Staff**	**Deadline**	**Responsible Person**
	Using E-mail Lists	Marketing Team		
	Software Training	Marketing Team and Other Staff as Necessary		
	Web Site Design	Marketing Team		
	Online Newsletters	Marketing Team		
	Online Fundraising	Development Staff		

● FORM1002.DOC

Form 10-3 Technology Checklist

Y	Activity	Rationale	Deadline	Responsible Person
	Check your web site for currency at least monthly.	If you have dead links, your visitor frustration goes way up.		
	Look into associations with other like organizations; cross link with trade associations.	The more ways people have to find you, the more people will find you!		
	Look into affiliations with commercial sites such as Amazon.com.	This brings in revenue and offers books, tapes, etc. in your area of interest for your visitors. It is an internal political decision. You may not want to commercialize your site, and the income is unrelated, and thus you have to report it on your annual IRS 990T report.		
	Is there a feedback loop on the web site?	Not hard, but make sure someone checks this e-mail regularly, or has it automatically forwarded to the correct person.		
	Is there a way for people to donate funds online?	Gotta do this if you have any significant fund-raising at all.		
	Do you have an online newsletter?	A great way to get news easily, cheaply, and fast to a huge and growing market.		

Form 10-3   Technology Checklist *(continued)*

Y	Activity	Rationale	Deadline	Responsible Person
	Do you have board and staff specific sections of your web site?	Get 'em, and get 'em now. They are easy to set up and password, and attend to the communications and information needs of two crucial markets.		
	Do you offer online payment and/or invoicing?	Ask your key payers if this works for them Talk to your bank about waiving online fees if your checking account balance stays high enough.		

FORM1003.DOC

Form 10-4 **Implementation Checklist**
Topic: Technology

Measurable Outcome	Deadline	Person or Group Responsible

⬤ FORM1004.DOC

D. ☞ HANDS-ON

☞ **HANDS-ON:** Spend some time learning how to search on the Internet and getting a listing of the places you have available to look. Use your bookmarking function (in Netscape Navigator) and Favorites function (in Internet Explorer) to keep a listing of good sites for funding, best practices, and competition research. If there is someone on your staff who is particularly adept at efficiently finding things for you, don't just delegate all your research work to them—do the searching with them, letting them mentor you in how to navigate the often-confusing maze of Web search options. And, there is good news: the next iteration of the Internet—more user friendly and more responsive, called the "semantic web"—is due to be up and running by 2006. So, there is hope if you are not a tech lover.

☞ **HANDS-ON:** E-mail should be a *supplement,* not a *substitute,* for communication. Always remember that there will be, at least for the foreseeable future, people who are involved with your organization who do not have access to e-mail or do not have access to it 24 hours a day (for example, staff who only use e-mail at work). And, don't assume that people check their e-mail four times a day. I regularly get surprised by people who only check their e-mail once a week or even once a month.

☞ **HANDS-ON:** If you don't have e-mail as an organization, let me be direct: get it, get it now, and get an individual e-mail address for every staff member. It is not expensive; it is the expectation of your customers; and it is the best way to go to use this increasingly important tool.

☞ **HANDS-ON:** Don't fall victim to what I call ego tech: giving everyone on your staff a phone and a pager. While the cost of technology has fallen dramatically, it is not free. Good stewardship decisions require that we look and see who really needs the equipment and regularly review that need. Look at the phone bills for all your organizational cell phones. How often are they being used? Who is calling whom? Does the phone get used enough to merit its monthly fee? The same goes for pagers. Although not telecommunications, *personal digital assistants* (PDAs) also can fall into the ego-tech trap. Make sure you *need* the tools for which you are paying.

☞ **HANDS-ON:** Check the available technology regularly—particularly in this area. Often, the phones and pagers are free with a 12-month contract. For example, one client of mine with 10 different facilities in one community has changed the communications devices for their four maintenance staff from pagers to cell phones and finally to cell phones with two-way radio capability (think a phone/walkie-talkie combination) over the past five years. The cost for outfitting four staff members with these immediate access tools is now less than it was for one pager five years ago.

☞ **HANDS-ON:** Speaking of price, check these out, too. Have your financial staff person or tech person call your cell phone and pager provider every 3-6 months and ask for the best rate. I tell all my clients to perform this task, and they regularly e-mail me with thanks because their costs get reduced by 10-50 percent with an increase in minutes, fees for long distance, and so on. If you haven't checked in the past half year, do so *today*.

☞ **HANDS-ON:** Do you have voice mail on your phone system? You should. Now, how easy is it for people to access it? Try this exercise: after hours, call your system and time how long it is before you can actually leave a message. How long are the verbal instructions at each step? How long is the personal message that your staff members leave? Shorten this time as much as possible. Voice mail is essential in customer satisfaction efforts, so try not to make your customers mad by making it inaccessible.

☞ **HANDS-ON:** Do NOT just survey someone in an e-mail. If you list a series of questions in an e-mail, people get confused in their reply, and what you get back is also sometimes garbled or confusing. There might be karets (>>>) in front of each line, or you might **bold** your questions to make it easier to read and then the reader's software doesn't support bold or prints the HTML code, and so on. So, here is the solution: use the e-mail to ask for someone's input, and then right in the e-mail provide a link to a web site (usually a hidden part of yours) that is a page set up as a survey with entry boxes and so on. This kind of site-based survey helps the person being surveyed enter data more easily, and as an extra benefit it collates and tabulates the data automatically. There are sites that do this kind of surveying for you, such as *www.statpac.com/online-surveys* or *http://free-online-surveys.co.uk,* and software exists that you can use as well. Also, if you are interested in this option, you may want to talk to your Internet Service Provider (ISP) to see if they offer surveying tabulation.

☞ **HANDS-ON:** Set up a special e-mail account for customer feedback. Most ISPs will let you route a special e-mail address, such as "*feedback@(your address)*," to a particular staff person's e-mail account. Using such an address alerts the staff person that this information is customer input and should be dealt with quickly. It also removes the responsibility from the person giving you input from having to put a particular item in the subject line of the e-mail. Whoever has the responsibility to deal with feedback should check e-mail at least twice a day and route the input as appropriate to other staff.

☞ **HANDS-ON:** When was the last time you called in to your organization and tried to go through the entire process (no shortcuts, assuming you are a new caller)? Do this today. Time yourself; how long does it take until you actually can start talking and leaving your message? Now, do the same thing again for someone who knows your extension. How long now? For new callers, no more than 30 seconds is acceptable; for people who know your extension, 10 seconds max. This may well mean that you have to change the greeting, both at the agency entry level and at your own mailbox. Remember, always have a live person answer the phone during office hours, but make the recorded part as easy as possible.

☞ **HANDS-ON:** As of this writing, I am not impressed at all with the collective donation sites on the Internet. These are places where you can list your organization, and any donations will come to you (minus, of course, a small fee). The literature on this topic, although preliminary, is not good, and my anecdotal evidence from my client organizations and people who come to my training sessions is disappointing to say the least. The rationale to join these groups, at least as far as I can tell, is to avoid having to pay credit card fees and set up the donation capability on your web site. These costs are not that big—certainly not for an organization with a significant development component.

E. FORMS ON THE COMPANION CD-ROM

Form 10-5 Forms on the Companion CD-ROM

Form Name	Form No.	Workbook Page	File Name	File Format
Technology Self-Assessment	10-1	100	FORM1001.DOC	Word for Windows
Technology Training Checklist	10-2	101	FORM1002.DOC	Word for Windows
Technology Checklist	10-3	102–103	FORM1003.DOC	Word for Windows
Implementation Checklist	10-4	104	FORM1004.DOC	Word for Windows
Forms on the Companion CD-ROM	10-5	107	FORM1005.DOC	Word for Windows

FORM1005.DOC

F. RESOURCES FOR FURTHER STUDY

Topic: Technology
Books
Here's the link for the John Wiley & Sons' web site for nonprofit technology. This way, you get the latest list: *www.wiley.com/remsearch.cgi?query=nonprofit+technology&field=keyword*
Software
Check it out—an index of software just for nonprofits:*www.npinfotech.org/tnopsi/* Another listing from TechSoup—these are mostly downloadable applications: *www.techsoup.org/sub_downloads.cfm?cg=nav&sg=resources_dl* Another listing from NonProfit expert—this one is deep and wide: *www.nonprofitexpert.com/nonprofit_software.htm* This listing is from About.com—warning: lots of popup ads: *http://nonprofit.about.com/cs/software*
Web Sites
Ninth Bridge *www.ninthbridge.org/* This group helps nonprofits with their technology issues. Nonprofit marketing: These two links are great places to learn more about marketing ideas and applications on the Web: *http://nonprofit.about.com/cs/npomarketing* *www.nonprofits.org/npofaq/keywords/2n.html* Also go to my web site links area for updated technology marketing links: *www.missionbased.com/links.htm*
Online Courses
Nonprofit Self-Grassroots MBA This online set of classes is designed for you to take at your own speed, and it covers all kinds of management skills, including marketing: *www.mapnp.org/library/mgmnt/mba_prog.htm*

11

Incredible Customer Service

Customer service-actually as you know I want you to go for customer *satisfaction!* Here's the scoop from *Mission-Based Marketing*.

A. STRAIGHT FROM *MISSION-BASED MARKETING*

If you spend tons of time figuring out who your markets are, segmenting them, finding out what they want, and then matching those wants up with your core competencies, you can still screw the marketing thing up. How? By not paying attention to ongoing customer service. Remember early in this workbook, and right at the beginning of *Mission Based Marketing,* I told you that market-driven not-for-profits realize that *everyone* is a customer (even the people who pay you). So, customer service is essential. Here are some ideas from *Mission-Based Marketing* on this important component of successful marketing.

Three Customer Service Rules

I've only said this about twenty times so far, but it can't be said enough: your environment today requires that you, your staff, and your volunteers treat everyone well and everyone like a customer, even though you might have never thought of them as anything but the enemy. You simply have to treat everyone—staff, board, volunteers, service recipients, and funders—like a customer if you are going to succeed as an organization in today's economic and political reality.

   We've discussed everyone being a customer, but it is so important (and so often ignored by not-for-profits) that I want to go through it again—this time with some ideas for how to bring your staff and board along for the ride. Let's review the three core rules of excellent services to all of your customers:

1. "The customer is not always right, but the customer is always the customer—so fix the problem."
2. "Customers never have problems; they always have crises, so fix the problem NOW."
3. "Never settle for good customer service. You should always seek total customer *satisfaction.*"

Success in the area of customer service (and customer satisfaction) starts with those three statements—not, of course, with just making the statements, but with believing them—and with structuring your organization to accommodate them.

First, of course, you must look at *everyone* as a customer. I know that this is a real stretch for many readers and a nearly insurmountable one for certain staff and board. For you, it might be difficult to think of your board as customers when they have always seemed like a group of nice, but sometime meddlesome, burdens. It might be tough to equate staff, who you are supposed to monitor, supervise, and (sometimes) discipline, as customers. It might be a challenge to think of a funder as a customer at all, particularly if you have spent the past 15 years fighting with them over regulations, funding criteria, and oversight.

But they all *are* customers. That is why they made the list of key markets in Chapter 6. You can choose to treat them as such and have a much higher likelihood of success. Or, you can treat them like you always have and increase your troubles markedly. I will assume for the rest of the chapter (in fact, for the rest of the book) that you will make the effort for the benefit of your organization and of the people you serve.

So, everyone is the customer. The customer can make mistakes, but the customer is still and always the customer. Sometimes they are happy, and sometimes not.

Let's look at each of the rules in much more detail.

> *"The customer is not always right, but the customer is always the customer—so fix the problem."*

Really, we get back to good management here. After nearly three decades in non-profit management and consulting, I know the single most important thing managers need to do with their staff is to *always tell them the truth.* You do not need to tell your staff everything, but it does mean that *everything you tell them should be absolutely fact, no exceptions, no exaggerations, and no talking the talk and not walking the walk.* What does that have to do with marketing? Lots, and here it impacts the way we motivate our staff. The old adage that "The customer is always right" is patently false, and we all know it. All of us know that we are not perfect. We all make mistakes. We also know that we are customers for many organizations and businesses. Thus, as customers, we are fallible. Your customers are the same: imperfect. In organizations that continue to tell their staff the old fable that the customer is always right, I have seen tremendous resentment against both management *and customers* build in employees. To say the least, this situation is counterproductive. A much more sensible way to look at it is that even though they might be wrong at times, their perspective is what counts. They *are* the customer, so make it right.

Taking this attitude with staff encourages them to overcome their natural resentment toward a customer who whines or complains inappropriately, but it also lets *them* know that *you* understand what they are going through.

> *"Customers never have problems; they always have crises, so fix the problem NOW."*

This can be the most mission-driven part of the three-part customer service maxim. From the customer's perspective, if they have a problem, it is not mundane or run-of-the-mill; it is one-of-a-kind, and it is theirs. If you or your staff, simply because you see this certain kind of problem all the time, treat it as no big deal, you will not address it quickly or with the empathy it deserves. We have all experienced this scenario personally from the point of view of the customer.

In most cases I have seen where customers are unhappy, the *perspectives of the customer* who we discussed earlier had not been trained and regularly reinforced. You might see 50 sick people today, but their illness is their only one. You might have 150 irrational customers returning things, but what they want is to (a:) gripe and (b:) get their money back or a working product. Do both and soon. You might see cars like these all the time, but we need to get the customer on her way as soon as possible.

And here is the mission driven part of this: For all the people who seek services, we need to have that sense of *compassionate urgency* I talked about earlier. We can't let the fact that we've helped 500 or 50,000 people with the same problem before make us take any customer, patient, student, parent, parishioner, or other user of our services for granted.

☐ **FOR EXAMPLE:** The best single illustration that I have ever seen is a television commercial for our local hospital-based cardiac unit. The commercial is pretty standard, with a physician telling you why the unit is so good, a few visuals of the high-tech environment, and so on. The cardiologist who does the commercial is a friend of mine, and after I saw the commercial the first time I asked him whether the tag line I liked so much was his creation or some marketing consultant's. "No," he said, "that is something we say every day in our staff meeting." And the line? "We need to remember that *what we do every day* here is a *once-in-a-lifetime experience* for our patients."

I have never seen it put better. Good marketing is a good mission. Your customers have to know you care and that you care about them, their issues, their family, and their problem. And if they do, they will return for more services and send others as well.

Now you know that every customer problem is a crisis, not just a problem. You might feel that you solve customer concerns quickly and efficiently, but does everyone else? You might feel that they do, and here is the test. Ask yourself this question: when I am out of town for two or three days, or on vacation for a week, things break, stuff goes wrong, and customers have problems. What happens then? Do my staff fix the problems, or do they wait for me to come back?

If you have told staff to fix customers' problems, do you then upbraid them about their solution? If so, they won't take such a risk again, and your customer will be poorly served. Staff must be empowered to fix customers' problems. They must be coached, encouraged, shown how, and then entrusted to fix things when Mr. Murphy arrives, because he will.

The bottom line question here is, "Do you really *empower* your staff to fix problems or just tell them to and then not support them?" Empowerment means to delegate *and* support staff in their customer relations. It means that customer satisfaction is an organizational priority for everyone and that you, as a supervisor, will go just as far to support a staff person in his or her customer relations as you will to actually satisfy the customer.

Let's face it. This activity is risky. All delegation is. But you need to have the attitude that you, as well as everyone else, learn from trying and often learn best by making mistakes. Just the way competition is risky, so is letting staff fix problems in your absence. But if you encourage innovation, encourage initiative, coach and support your staff, and train them in the outcomes you want, then most people will rise to the occasion. You will find that some, perhaps many, of your staff have different ways of solving a problem—of meeting a want—than you do. And often, you will find that those solutions are *better* than yours (which is OK).

Begin or expand your delegation with the understanding that the alternative is much more dangerous. If you don't delegate customer service, if you don't make sure that everyone is empowered to fix customer problems, and if you make every issue wait for you to intervene personally, you will absolutely be losing customers. A competitive environment doesn't wait for you to personally get involved in every decision. It moves on. Empower your people to fix problems (oops, crises!), and fix them *now*.

B. BASELINE SELF-ASSESSMENT

Form 11-1 Customer Service Self-Assessment	Yes	No
Do all of our staff get at least two hours of customer service training annually?	3	–2
Do we train our staff to have a sense of compassionate urgency about everyone we serve?	3	0
Do our staff understand that everyone is a customer, including our funders?	2	–2
Do we tell our staff that while customers may not always be right, they are customers, so fix the problem and fix it now?	2	–1
Do we empower them to fix these problems?	3	–2
Do we focus on customer satisfaction as opposed to customer service?	2	0
Do we have a system that provides staff information and feedback on customer complaints?	2	–1
Do we survey our funders to assure their satisfaction at least annually?	2	–1
Do we visit key staff at their place of business at least annually?	3	–1
Total of Column Score (Add up each column and put the answer here.) ➜		
TOTAL SCORE (Add total scores from Yes and No columns and put the answer here.) ➜		

 FORM1101.DOC

SCORING ANALYSIS:

18–22 Excellent
13–17 Very Good
10–12 Adequate
Less than 10—You need to look at customer service, look at it hard, and soon.

C. WORKSHEETS AND CHECKLISTS

Form 11-2 Training Checklist—Customer Service

Y	Training Type	For Which Staff	Deadline	Responsible Person
	Customer Service	All Staff—annually		
	Building Customer Loyalty	Marketing Team		
	Handling Customer Complaints	Marketing Team		

FORM1102.DOC

Form 11-3 **Marketing Checklist—Customer Service**

Y	Activity	Rationale	Deadline	Responsible Person
	Have all staff take customer service training.	It's important that everyone understand the three basics. Having everyone take the training also underscores that everyone is on the marketing team.		
	Develop a good customer complaint feedback loop.	Assures that the marketing team is tracking problems, and that they are getting resolved.		
	Build satisfaction assessment into service.	Make sure people ask, "was there anything else we could do to improve our service?" to every customer every time.		
	Maximize the ways people can ask for improvement.	Online, in person, in writing, or through surveys. The more ways people have to ask for improvements the more they will.		
	Empower and require staff to fix problems fast.	Customers only have crises! And you can't be everywhere all the time.		

FORM1103.DOC

Form 11-4 Implementation Checklist Topic: Marketing		
Measurable Outcome	**Deadline**	**Person or Group Responsible**

● FORM1104.DOC

D. ☞ HANDS-ON

☞ **HANDS-ON:** If you didn't use the hands on suggestion earlier, now is a good time. Find a friend who is willing to come in to your organization as a potential customer. Ask him or her to come in at their convenience and to take notes of everything that they see that they like and everything that they see that they dislike—even in the slightest way. Pick a friend who you feel will be tough on your organization, and emphasize to him or her that you want to improve things. After the visit, have your friend list the good and bad parts of the visit, and if he or she is willing, do the "debrief" with your marketing team or management team. It will be an eye-opener, I assure you.

☞ **HANDS-ON:** When dealing with an unhappy customer, follow this checklist:

- *First, listen to their whole complaint.* Do not interrupt, cut them off, or in any way impede them from venting. If they are mad enough to complain, they want their whole say. Don't make them madder by correcting, interrupting, or explaining—at least not until they are through. Let them finish, *then* ask your clarification questions.

- *Second, acknowledge the customer's perspective.* Here, there are two possibilities: the customer is correct and you have messed up, or the customer is wrong and you haven't. In either case, it is crucial that you acknowledge their perspective. First, if the customer is correct, say, "Mr. Jones, it sounds like our mistake. I apologize, and I really appreciate the fact that you took the time to call." Or, the customer is not right and you say: "Mr. Jones, I understand your frustration and I'm sorry you feel that way. I appreciate your letting us know about the situation." Acknowledge that you heard their problem, and sympathize with their feelings. Make sure they know you heard them.

- *Third, ask them what they want.* Here is the place most of us mess up. We offer a solution to an unhappy person without asking *what they want*. Ask first, "Now, what can we do to make this right with you, Mr. Jones?" If they don't know what they want, then offer a suggestion. More often that not, they really don't want anything other than to feel better and for the problem not to reoccur. Ask first.

- *Fourth, never make promises you cannot keep.* As helping people, we want to make our customers happy. One way we think we can do that is by giving them *anything* that they want. It makes them happy now but really unhappy later when we can't deliver. When you say, "We'll have the material mailed to you today," "We'll be able to make your first appointment in a week," or "Check in for a first time client only takes 30 minutes," are all of these absolutely true? Can you do what you say, and to the letter? If not, don't say it, and make sure that all of your staff understand. Here is an area where the person on the line of service can really make headaches for you. Tell your staff to make only promises you can keep. And, here's a promise that's easy to make but impossible to keep: "Mr. Jones, I promise this will *never happen again*." Has anyone ever heard of Murphy's Law?

- *Fifth, keep excellent notes.* Particularly if you have a customer problem, keep excellent notes about what was said, who promised whom what, by when, and so on. Documentation not only protects you, but it also *reminds* you of what your obligations are, making it more likely that you will keep your promises. It also provides a means by which you can share the complaint with other staff members to assure that the problem you just dealt with doesn't get repeated elsewhere.

- *Sixth, never assume that a customer is happy.* Ask. Measure. Interview. If you do have a complaint, call those who complain yourself. This action alone will diffuse 90 percent of complaints. But don't wait for them to complain—only 10 percent of people do and the other 90 percent (that don't) tell 10 other people and *exaggerate their problem*. So, get out ahead of the customer problem. Ask, ask, and ask.

☞ **HANDS-ON:** NEVER, EVER, EVER assume that a customer, even one who has an intimate knowledge of your organization, its core competencies, and all of its services, can or will connect their problem to your solution. They *might,* but more often they won't. Don't sit back and wait for them to come to you. Go to them. Ask, listen, and respond. This type of asking is best done informally or in focus groups, as we discussed in Chapter 8, and all of your staff need to be part of the culture of asking. I see too many organizations that are stunned when people go elsewhere for services because "they know about us." Well, perhaps they do, but do they know (or remember) what you can do for them and for their problems? Obviously not.

E. FORMS ON THE COMPANION CD-ROM

Form 11-5 Forms on the Companion CD-ROM

Form Name	Form No.	Workbook Page	File Name	File Format
Customer Service Self-Assessment	11-1	112	FORM1101.DOC	Word for Windows
Training Checklist— Customer Service	11-2	113	FORM1102.DOC	Word for Windows
Marketing Checklist— Customer Service	11-3	114	FORM1103.DOC	Word for Windows
Implementation Checklist	11-4	115	FORM1104.DOC	Word for Windows
Forms on the Companion CD-ROM	11-5	117	FORM1105.DOC	Word for Windows

FORM1105.DOC

F. RESOURCES FOR FURTHER STUDY

Topic: Customer Service
Books
Marketing Nonprofit Programs and Services: Proven and Practical Strategies to Get More Customers, Members, and Donors by Douglas B. Herron. Cloth. Jossey-Bass, October 1996. *Managing to Keep the Customer: How to Achieve and Maintain Superior Customer Service Throughout the Organization, Revised Edition,* by Robert L. Desatnick and Denis H. Detzel. Cloth. Jossey-Bass, May 1993.
Software
None that I know of.
Web Sites
The free management library on customer service: *www.mapnp.org/library/customer/satisfy.htm*
Online Courses
Nonprofit Self-Grassroots MBA This online set of classes is designed for you to take at your own speed, and it covers all kinds of management skills, including marketing: *www.mapnp.org/library/mgmnt/mba_prog.htm*

12

A Marketing Planning Process

Planning how to get all your work done and how to fit it all into everything else you, your staff, and your board have to do is crucial. Frankly, if you don't have a plan, it probably won't get done. Here's the way to accomplish your tasks, straight from *Mission-Based Marketing:*

A. STRAIGHT FROM *MISSION-BASED MARKETING*

Now, it is time to put it all together in a plan that will help you assure that things actually get done and that will enable you to budget time and dollars and focus on the marketing effort. Here are some suggestions directly from *Mission-Based Marketing*.

Developing Your Marketing Team

You already know that marketing is everyone's job, not just the executive director's or the director of marketing's. Everyone is part of the marketing effort, but not everyone can sit on the committee, or team, that develops and implements your marketing plan.

You do need a team, however, and you need it to be broad-based and with a variety of experience and perspective. You need the team to develop the marketing plans, to develop your asking, to allocate the marketing portion of your budget, and to do the lion's share of the regular customer contact. Let's look at the makeup of the marketing team and then review its responsibilities. I think you will find that by developing such a team, you will greatly improve the results of your marketing efforts.

1. Who should be on the marketing team?

I always like teams or committees that are broadly based. Thus, I do not think that this group should be just board members, nor do I support teams that are only made up of senior management staff. Think of your organizational chart. It has vertical levels (senior management, mid management, and line staff) and horizontal dimensions (varying programs or areas of service). I have found that a wide representation of your organization, both vertically and horizontally, benefits everyone the best. You get input from all areas and grow your future leaders. If you believe me when I tell you that marketing is a team effort and that everyone is on the marketing team, make sure you put those words into action when you develop the organization's marketing team. These people need to be involved:

- *CEO*. The top staff person in the organization needs to be involved, at least in the selection of target markets, marketing planning, and other strategic issues. He or she probably shouldn't chair the committee, though.

- *Board member.* You should ask one or two members of the board to be involved in this critical part of the organization, particularly if you have a board member who is involved in marketing in his or her regular job.

- *Marketing director.* Whichever person on your staff has the core responsibility for marketing should not only be on the committee, but he or she should most likely chair it.

- *Director(s) of services.* Whether this title is one or more staff members, the people in charge of your core services need to be part of the asking and the listening.

- *Mid-level and line staff.* You need people from throughout the organization. Many of these people have more direct contact with your customers than senior management; thus, their input is critical. It is also a great staff development experience for them.

- *Outside expert.* Some organizations find it helpful to have one or two outsiders on the marketing team—almost always people who have specific expertise to offer.

The team should probably not be any larger than 10 to 12 people or much smaller than 5 to 6. That is the best size for a working group such as this one.

2.   *What are the marketing team's responsibilities?*

Once you gather your group, what do you have to do? The following is a list of outcomes that the marketing team should consider:

- Develop a marketing plan coordinated with the organization strategic plan. This plan should include strategic as well as one-year goals, objectives, and desired outcomes.

- Develop and administer a marketing budget.

- Develop a schedule of organizational asking.

- Develop and keep up-to-date all organizational marketing material.

- Develop and keep up-to-date the organization's "look" and logo.

- Monitor trends in the industry and advise the board and management team as appropriate.

- Implement adequate surveying, focus groups, and interviewing to stay in constant touch with the wants of the markets.

- Sponsor in-house training as appropriate on customer service, marketing, asking, and other related subjects for all staff.

- Keep in regular personal contact with key market segments.

- Regularly train to further the staff's own marketing expertise. Get outside education for team members on surveying, interviewing, market analysis, and materials development. Develop internal expertise.

I know that these tasks sound like a lot to do. But if the group meets every two weeks (for two to three hours) for the first six months and then monthly on a permanent basis, there should be adequate time to get it all done. And, to get you jump started, I have broken out some crucial things you need to get accomplished in your first six months.

3. Outcomes for the first six months

The following are some suggestions of things that your marketing team can strive for in your first six months:

- *Attain common ground*. It is important that you come to a common ground on definitions and methods on achieving common goals. I would suggest that you have all team members read this book. If you find it helpful, you can use the *Mission-Based Marketing Discussion Leader's Guide,* which is designed for groups just like your marketing team.

- *Identify your target markets*. Go through the market identification process that you learned about in Chapter 4. Work toward a consensus on who your target markets arc.

- *Identify a contact for each target market*. Where possible, identify an individual at each of your target markets with whom you will keep in regular contact. This identification is easier for a funder and more difficult for a target market such as "teenagers" or "nursing home residents," but even within those broad markets there will be representatives, advocates, family members, or others who can fill that role.

- *Assign a team member to each target market segment*. Each member of the team will have at least one (and probably more than one) market on which to focus. This experience will develop into expertise over time—something you will really want to have.

- *Develop benchmarks*. Where you can, look at the status of these markets now. In many cases, you will already have internal data you can look at. How large is the market? How many customers return? Where are our referrals from? How happy are the markets with us? How many complaints do we get? How much staff or board turnover do we have? What are the levels of customer satisfaction now? All of this information goes into your benchmark setting. These benchmarks will be your starting point for improvement, because if you don't set them now, you won't be able to tell later how far you have come.

- *Develop an asking schedule.* See Section B in this chapter for more on how and why to develop an asking schedule. You need to coordinate your asking *now*, not later.

- *Develop a rough draft marketing plan.* See Section D for more. Suffice it to say that in six months you will be pressed to do all of these items *and* develop a plan, but you can develop some goals and outcomes.

Your marketing team is a crucial component of your overall marketing effort. Choose the people carefully; give them support and resources (including time away from their other duties); and make marketing a priority for them. Don't try to do this task with one or two already overworked staff people. Get a group, motivate it, support it, and have high expectations of it.

B. BASELINE SELF-ASSESSMENT

Form 12-1 **Marketing Planning Self-Assessment**		
	Yes	**No**
Do we have a current marketing plan (3 to 5 years)?	**3**	**–1**
Are both board *and* staff involved in the marketing planning process?	**2**	**–1**
Do we float drafts of our plan widely both inside and outside the organization?	**3**	**–1**
Does our planning process include the people we serve, the funding sources, and the community?	**2**	**–1**
Do we regularly review progress at implementing the marketing plan at staff and board meetings?	**2**	**0**
Are our marketing goals and objectives part of our strategic plan?	**2**	**0**
Does our marketing plan delineate our target markets, our core competencies, and how we plan to meet our markets' wants?	**3**	**–2**
Is our marketing plan included in our strategic plan?	**2**	**–1**
Are adequate funds budgeted for our marketing priorities, including asking, training, and marketing materials?	**3**	**–2**
Is marketing an organizational priority for staff and board?	**4**	**–2**
Total of Column Score (Add up each column and put the answer here.) ➔		
TOTAL SCORE (Add total scores from Yes and No columns and put the answer here.) ➔		

● FORM1201.DOC

SCORING ANALYSIS:

21–26 Excellent
15–20 Very Good
10–14 Adequate
Less than 10—Watch out. You might be tempted not to put your work into a plan.
Don't give in to that temptation.

Planning is the best way to assure implementation. The process of planning itself often takes the bugs out of the best of systems and intentions. It also helps you estimate costs much better and will involve your marketing team, board, and community—thus helping bring everyone onto the marketing team.

C. WORKSHEETS AND CHECKLISTS

Form 12-2   A Marketing Plan Outline

This is a sample of a marketing planning outline for you to consider.

1. Your Mission Statement

2. Executive Summary

A brief summary of the marketing plan including a list of your target markets and core competencies, and how they match up with the wants of the markets.

3. Introduction and Purpose of the Plan

A rationale for the uses of the plan. This section can also include a brief recitation of the planning process and its level of inclusion.

4. Description of the Markets

A full description of your major markets, their wants, their numbers, and projected growth or reduction in demand from these markets.

5. Description of the Services

A description of each of your services, including number of people served, service area or criteria for service, and any accreditation that these services may have earned.

6. Analysis of Market Wants

A review of the surveys, interviews, or focus groups that you do to prepare the plan. The wants of the markets and how they match up to your core competencies should be included here.

7. Target Markets and Rationale

Out of all your potential markets, you will choose a few priority targets. Describe them here in more detail along with your reasoning for their prioritization.

8. Marketing Goals and Objectives

The goals, objectives, and (for annual plans) action steps that will get your marketing strategies implemented.

9. Appendices

Minimal supporting information for the plan.

FORM1202.DOC

Form 12-3   An Asking Schedule

Enter your markets into this form, and then agree on how you will survey and how often (the Cycle).

Method	Market	Cycle	Deadline for this year
Survey			
Email Input			
Focus Group			
Interview (formal)			
Interview (informal)			

FORM1203.DOC

Form 12-4   Marketing Checklist—Planning

Y	Activity	Rationale	Deadline	Responsible Person
	Identify our Marketing Team.	You need the team. Get one now from a diverse cross section of your organization.		
	Set our goals for the first six months.	Look in Chapter 12, pages 217–218, of *Mission-Based Marketing* for some reasonable outcomes.		
	Develop an asking schedule.	Don't ask too often or too infrequently. This schedule will keep you on track.		
	Develop a draft marketing plan.	Start with some goals and objectives.		
	Float the draft for comment.	This will get good ideas and develop ownership among the staff and board.		
	Finalize the plan and get it included in the organizational strategic plan.	This coordinates marketing with other activities.		

FORM1204.DOC

Form 12-5 **Implementation Checklist** **Topic: Planning**		
Measurable Outcome	**Deadline**	**Person or Group Responsible**

● FORM1205.DOC

D. ☞ HANDS-ON

☞ **HANDS-ON:** As I noted in Chapter 8, one of the advantages of asking regularly is that you can measure trends. But how often is often enough? There is a balance between surveying all the time and surveying once a millennium. My general guidelines are:

- *Staff surveys*. Every 18 months—which gives you enough time to implement appropriate suggestions and have them take effect

- *Consumer surveys*. Some people survey annually, some every six months. It will depend on your type of services. A school might formally survey the parents and students semi-annually while a symphony might ask its patrons only once in a strategic planning cycle. Generally, I would say annually.

- *Funders*. Annually or at the end of each funding cycle

- *Donors*. Every two years or at the point of the analysis of a large capital campaign

- *Referrers*. Every six months

☞ **HANDS-ON:** When you develop asking materials and reports (such as a report of a survey), put right on the cover of the report the date that it was administered *and the* *date of the next surveying*. For example, if I surveyed staff to ascertain their job satisfaction, I might put down that the survey was completed in June 2003 with a update of the survey due in two years, or June 2005. By putting the deadline of the update on the report, you are more likely to remember to do the survey again.

E. FORMS ON THE COMPANION CD-ROM

Form 12-6 **Forms on the Companion CD-ROM**				
Form Name	**Form No.**	**Workbook Page**	**File Name**	**File Format**
Planning Self-Assessment	12-1	123	FORM1201.DOC	Word for Windows
A Sample Marketing Plan Outline	12-2	124	FORM1202.DOC	Word for Windows
Developing an Asking Schedule	12-3	125	FORM1203.DOC	Word for Windows
Checklist for Planning	12-4	126	FORM1204.DOC	Word for Windows
Implementation Checklist	12-5	127	FORM1205.DOC	Word for Windows
Forms on the Companion CD-ROM	12-6	128	FORM1206.DOC	Word for Windows

FORM1206.DOC

F. RESOURCES FOR FURTHER STUDY

Topic: Marketing Planning

Books

Developing a Winning Marketing Plan by William A. Cohen. Cloth. John Wiley & Sons, April 1987. US $42.50.

The Marketing Plan, 2nd Edition, by William A. Cohen. Paper. John Wiley & Sons, July 1997. US $44.95.

Planning Your Internet Marketing Strategy: A Doctor Ebiz Guide by Ralph F. Wilson. Paper. John Wiley & Sons, October 2001.

Marketing Workbook for Nonprofit Organizations: Mobilize People for Marketing Success by Gary J. Stern. Wiler Foundation, March 2001.

Software

Marketing Planning Software:
Market Plan Pro, Palo Alto Software, *www.paloalto.com*

Web Sites

The Free Management Library on marketing planning:
www.mapnp.org/library/mrktng/planning/planning.htm

Online Courses

Nonprofit Self-Grassroots MBA This online set of classes is designed for you to take at your own speed, and it covers all kinds of management skills, including marketing:
www.mapnp.org/library/mgmnt/mba_prog.htm

Nonprofit education: This is the most complete site for nonprofit academic programs all over North America. Check out the institutions to find the most up-to-date online offerings, which are increasing every month:
http://pirate.shu.edu/~mirabero/Kellogg.html

About the CD-ROM

INTRODUCTION

The forms on the enclosed CD-ROM are saved in Microsoft Word for Windows version 7.0. In order to use the forms, you will need to have word processing software capable of reading Microsoft Word for Windows version 7.0 files.

SYSTEM REQUIREMENTS

- IBM PC or compatible computer
- CD-ROM drive
- Windows 95 or later
- Microsoft Word for Windows version 7.0 (including the Microsoft converter*) or later or other word processing software capable of reading Microsoft Word for Windows 7.0 files.

*Word 7.0 needs the Microsoft converter file installed in order to view and edit all enclosed files. If you have trouble viewing the files, download the free converter from the Microsoft web site. The URL for the converter is: *http://office.microsoft.com/downloads/2000/wrd97cnv.aspx*.

Microsoft also has a viewer that can be downloaded, which allows you to view, but not edit documents. This viewer can be downloaded at: *http://office.microsoft.com/downloads/9798/wdvw9716.aspx*.

(NOTE: Many popular word processing programs are capable of reading Microsoft Word for Windows 7.0 files. However, users should be aware that a slight amount of formatting might be lost when using a program other than Microsoft Word.)

USING THE FILES

Loading Files

To use the files, launch your word processing program. Select **File, Open** from the pull-down menu. Select the appropriate drive and directory. A list of files should appear. If you do not see a list of files in the directory, you need to select **WORD DOCUMENT (*.DOC)** under **Files of Type.** Double click on the file you want to open. Edit the file according to your needs.

Printing Files

If you want to print the files, select **File, Print** from the pull-down menu.

Saving Files

When you have finished editing a file, you should save it under a new file name by selecting **File, Save As** from the pull-down menu.

USER ASSISTANCE

If you need assistance with installation or if you have a damaged CD-ROM, please contact Wiley Technical Support at:

Phone: 201-748-6753
Fax: 201-748-6450 (Attention: Wiley Technical Support)
URL: *www.wiley.com/techsupport*

To place additional orders or to request information about other Wiley products, please call 1-800-225-5945.

FORMS ON THE CD-ROM

Form Names	Form Nos.	Document Names
Self-Assessment—Flexibility	3-1	FORM0301.DOC
Self-Assessment—The Marketing Cycle	3-2	FORM0302.DOC
Self-Assessment—Market Identification	3-3	FORM0303.DOC
Self-Assessment—Your Competition	3-4	FORM0304.DOC
Self-Assessment—Asking Your Markets	3-5	FORM0305.DOC
Self-Assessment—Your Marketing Materials	3-6	FORM0306.DOC
Self-Assessment—Technology & Marketing	3-7	FORM0307.DOC
Self-Assessment—Incredible Customer Service	3-8	FORM0308.DOC
Self-Assessment—Marketing Planning	3-9	FORM0309.DOC
Self-Assessment—Scoring Compilation	3-10	FORM0310.DOC
Forms on the Companion CD-ROM	3-11	FORM0311.DOC
Flexibilty Self-Assessment	4-1	FORM0401.DOC
Flexiblity Checklist	4-2	FORM0402.DOC
Implementation Checklist	4-3	FORM0403.DOC
Forms on the Companion CD-ROM	4-4	FORM0404.DOC
Marketing Cycle Self-Assessment	5-1	FORM0501.DOC
Marketing Cycle Checklist	5-2	FORM0502.DOC
Market Identification	5-3	FORM0503.DOC
Implementation Checklist	5-4	FORM0504.DOC
Forms on the Companion CD-ROM	5-5	FORM0505.DOC
Who Are Our Markets?	6-1	FORM0601.DOC
Training Checklist—Marketing	6-2	FORM0602.DOC
Marketing Checklist—Target Market Identification	6-3	FORM0603.DOC

Form Names	Form Nos.	Document Names
What Do Our Markets Really Want?	6-4	FORM0604.DOC
Our Core Competencies	6-5	FORM0605.DOC
Implementation Checklist	6-6	FORM0606.DOC
Forms on the Companion CD-ROM	6-7	FORM0607.DOC
Competition Self-Assessment	7-1	FORM0701.DOC
Assessment of Competition	7-2	FORM0702.DOC
Checklist for Competition	7-3	FORM0703.DOC
Implementation Checklist	7-4	FORM0704.DOC
Forms on the Companion CD-ROM	7-5	FORM0705.DOC
Asking Self-Assessment	8-1	FORM0801.DOC
Checklist—Asking Informally	8-2	FORM0802.DOC
Checklist—Asking with Surveys	8-3	FORM0803.DOC
Sample Survey	8-4	FORM0804.DOC
Checklist—Asking Focus Groups	8-5	FORM0805.DOC
Implementation Checklist	8-6	FORM0806.DOC
Forms on the Companion CD-ROM	8-7	FORM0807.DOC
Marketing Materials Self-Assessment	9-1	FORM0901.DOC
Training Checklist—Marketing	9-2	FORM0902.DOC
Marketing Materials Checklist	9-3	FORM0903.DOC
Web Site Checklist	9-4	FORM0904.DOC
Implementation Checklist	9-5	FORM0905.DOC
Forms on the Companion CD-ROM	9-6	FORM0906.DOC
Technology Self-Assessment	10-1	FORM1001.DOC
Technology Training Checklist	10-2	FORM1002.DOC
Technology Checklist	10-3	FORM1003.DOC
Implementation Checklist	10-4	FORM1004.DOC
Forms on the Companion CD-ROM	10-5	FORM1005.DOC
Customer Service Self-Assessment	11-1	FORM1101.DOC
Training Checklist—Customer Service	11-2	FORM1102.DOC
Marketing Checklist—Customer Service	11-3	FORM1103.DOC
Implementation Checklist	11-4	FORM1104.DOC
Forms on the Companion CD-ROM	11-5	FORM1105.DOC
Planning Self-Assessment	12-1	FORM1201.DOC
A Sample Marketing Plan Outline	12-2	FORM1202.DOC
Developing an Asking Schedule	12-3	FORM1203.DOC
Checklist for Planning	12-4	FORM1204.DOC
Implementation Checklist	12-5	FORM1205.DOC
Forms on the Companion CD-ROM	12-6	FORM1206.DOC

Index

For information about the disk see the **About the CD-ROM** section on page 130.